THE TEN LARGEST
SUNDAY SCHOOLS

AND WHAT MAKES
THEM GROW

D1501235

THE TEN LARGEST
SUNDAY SCHOOLS

AND WHAT MAKES
THEM GROW

by Elmer L. Towns

BAKER BOOK HOUSE, Grand Rapids, Michigan

Table of Contents

34859

The material for this book is taken from an annual survey of the state of the Sunday schools in the United States compiled each year by *Christian Life* Magazine. The author is grateful for the cooperation of the editors of *Christian Life* magazine, denominational Sunday school secretaries, secretaries of area Sunday school associations, the staff of the National Sunday School Association and publishers of Sunday School Literature as well as many individual ministers and lay people interested in the Christian education program of the church.

Introduction

Why do some Sunday Schools grow in attendance at fantastic rates to unbelievable sizes, and others stagnate? Some Sunday Schools reach a vast number of people, win hundreds to Christ, and have a large teaching ministry. Others seem to die in the delivery room.

Why?

I have been in some churches that seem to have all the ingredients for expansion yet they remain inhibited year after year. Other churches I would write off the possibility list, stating, "They can't grow in that location or in that building." But they continue to expand.

Why?

What is the secret to Sunday School expansion? Is there some magical formula to be applied for growth? Does correct theological doctrine produce a rise in attendance figures? Many years ago I asked if there existed a set of laws that automatically built attendance when applied.

Years ago the Southern Baptist Convention released a filmstrip, *The Laws of Sunday School Growth,* that reflects the Convention's strategy for growth. These laws were restated by J. N. Barnette in his study book, *The Pull of the People,* Convention Press, 1956. Many Sunday School authorities outside the ten million member Southern Baptist Convention look to the laws of Sunday School growth as expressed by the Southern Baptist as an infallible guide to Sunday School expansion. Yet these laws of Sunday School growth are either ignored or broken by many of the ten largest Sunday Schools. In fact, most of the ten largest Sunday Schools in America do not follow these laws of Sunday School growth, yet continue to grow.

Why?

Six of the Sunday Schools among the ten largest are listed in the yearbook of The Baptist Bible Fellowship, Springfield, Missouri. Only one of the ten largest Sunday Schools is from a Southern Baptist Church. May we conclude that the Baptist Bible Fellowship has better laws for Sunday School growth, or that perhaps the laws for Sunday School growth as expressed by the Southern Baptist Convention are not as effective as once believed? Maybe the youthful enthusiasm of the Baptist Bible Fellowship produces more dedication and hard work than the older, more formal Southern Baptist Denomination. The Baptist Bible Fellowship does seem to be more effective in building larger Sunday Schools.

Why?

An interesting prediction was made by Dr. John Rawlings, minister of Landmark Baptist Temple, Cincinnati, Ohio, and Vice President of Baptist Bible College, Springfield, Missouri. He feels that in the next ten years the Baptist Bible Fellowship will have between twenty-five and fifty churches averaging over three thousand in Sunday School. Today, there are only seven Sunday Schools that average that high in attendance and five of these Sunday Schools are listed in the Baptist Bible Fellowship Yearbook. If the Baptist Bible Fellowship works as hard in the next ten years as it has in the past ten years it probably will prove Rawlings correct.

This book is written to help many struggling Sunday Schools wanting to grow. Small works drain the vision and enthusiasm of faithful lay workers and clergymen. Nothing is more discouraging than to pour energy, hope and prayers into a Sunday School, then see it defiantly refuse to expand. A stagnant Sunday School eats the heart and desire out of workers.

The example of these ten churches can help small Sunday Schools spot weaknesses and plan fruitful programs. Their principles of growth may rejuvenate a discouraged pastor, giving him a new vision of the work. A successful man surely does not follow the example of failure.

The author gets disturbed at some of the lectures given at Sunday School conventions and Christian education conferences. Speakers with little experience in building attendance at Sunday School give lectures on outreach and expansion. Principles are suggested to help Sunday Schools grow in attendance, when in fact, the application may deter the outreach and growth of a work. And then some people are up in the air. Ivory towers are fine, but very few people live there. Solid research is needed in Sunday School outreach and expansion.

I was greatly impressed with the ministers, staff and the congregations that I visited in the ten largest Sunday Schools project. Much is heard today about the dying church institution. The ten largest Sunday Schools have life, and you feel as if you are "where the action is" when you visit their services. The lost are being converted, prayers are being answered, and progress is evident. I wished I lived close enough so my family and I could attend one of these churches.

But I do not give a "blanket" approval to all I saw in the ten largest Sunday Schools. Some of the churches have features I think are not educationally sound. But this study is not to express my opinions. I have attempted to remain objective, and report the facts as they exist. The purpose of this study was to determine why these ten Sunday Schools became the largest in the United States — not to examine the all round effectiveness of their programs. I have not tried to criticize these Sunday Schools, but to communicate those principles that have caused them to grow.

You may read this book and immediately attempt to "apply" some of the principles. Be careful! Each practice must be taken in its total context. *You* may not be a Dr. Jack Hyles or Dr. Lee Roberson with a tremendous gift to motivate people. You may not be an organizer or financier, or have other gifts which characterize these men. Some of their success lies not in their principles but in the power of the personality behind the principle.

If you desire to build a large Sunday School, you might begin your ministry by working for an experienced pastor who is already building a large Sunday School. Spend three or four years in the "school of experience," studying the organization and the man who makes it grow. During your internship you will learn administration, self-discipline and technique. But the greatest lesson will be *vision.* The ability to think big is not learned in Bible College or Seminary. We learn vision by seeing the work of God through the eyes of a man of God.

At places the term *Sunday School* and *church* are interchanged in this manuscript and some book reviewer might criticize this study for confusing Sunday School and church. This interchange of terms is deliberate because in the thinking of some of the ministers in these churches, their Sunday School and church are one. Also, some of the policies set by the church (deacons) contribute directly to the Sunday School. Therefore, when the author lists the factors that cause growth, many of the principles from this study apply to the church rather than to the educational outreach of the Sunday School.

Some will be disappointed in the chapters on "Factors of Growth." Their disappointment will be caused by what was left out. There are many items (520 responses on the questionnaires) in these ten churches that contribute to efficient Sunday School organization, or sensible church management, but are left off the list of factors. Also, many items of educational techniques were left off the list of factors. This study was an attempt to determine the factors that caused the growth of the ten largest Sunday Schools. Factors that did not contribute to attendance growth were left off the list. This will account for an omission of some principles from the list.

Others may be disappointed in what is included. Several traditional sacred cows of Christian education are attacked. Small class grouping, and the Board of Christian Education are neglected, if not repudiated by these Sunday Schools. Paid staff workers instead of lay workers administer the Sunday School and seven Sunday Schools write a part of their own Sunday School literature, rather than purchase it from a publishing house. I have long felt that we need more research in Christian education, because much of what we do is motivated by tradition, rather than by principles that have been properly researched and tested.

I must extend appreciation to each of the ministers of the ten largest Sunday Schools. Their patience in answering questions and providing information is greatly appreciated. Their openness was needed to complete the study. They made staff members and secretaries available to help "run down facts." The spirit of Christian hospitality was greatly manifested. Also, the ministers and/or their staff read the chapter on their church and the chapters on Factors Causing Growth. Their approval of the facts and illustrations was needed to make the book more accurate. The author assumes responsibility for the inclusion of all material; the ministers verified the facts and their interpretation.

Dr. Harold Henniger of Canton Baptist Temple deserves special appreciation for contacting several other ministers in the ten largest Sunday schools, introducing me to them. I count it a privilege to have preached in Akron Baptist Temple, Canton Baptist Temple and Landmark Baptist Temple.

The original article on the ten largest Sunday Schools appeared in *Christian Life Magazine*, September, 1968. The author is grateful for the encouragement given him for the completion of this project.

The seminary students at Trinity Evangelical Divinity School have noted a change in my teaching since I undertook this study. I am more convinced of the effectiveness of church-centered evangelism than at any time in my ministry. I feel the future of the church is centered on the institutional church, and I am optimistic for its future. As a result of interviewing the ministers of these churches I feel I can trust God for greater work on this earth than I could previously. No one could become totally involved in the life of these churches, and not be a changed person. I am grateful for the privilege of doing this study and writing this book.

ELMER L. TOWNS
Associate Professor of Christian Education
Trinity Evangelical Divinity School

Sunday School Editor
Christian Life Magazine

AMERICA'S TEN LARGEST SUNDAY SCHOOLS, 1969

Sunday School Attendance

1. Akron Baptist Temple, Akron, Ohio . . . 5,762

2. Highland Park Baptist Church,
   Chattanooga, Tennessee 4,821**

3. First Baptist Church, Dallas, Texas . . . 4,731***

4. First Baptist Church, Hammond, Indiana . 3,978

5. Canton Baptist Temple, Canton, Ohio . . 3,581

6. Landmark Baptist Temple, Cincinnati, Ohio 3,540

7. Temple Baptist Church, Detroit, Michigan 3,400****

8. First Baptist Church, Van Nuys, California 2,847

9. Thomas Road Baptist Church,
   Lynchburg, Virginia 2,640

10. Calvary Temple, Denver, Colorado . . . 2,453

° Material in this book taken from a survey of 30 largest Sunday Schools in U.S. published and copyrighted annually in October, *Christian Life* magazine, Gundersen Dr. and Schmale Road, Wheaton, Illinois 60187.

** 42 chapels are added in the total attendnce.

*** 6 chapels are added in the total attendance.

****The average attendance was not available. The church responded that the Sunday school has averaged over 4,400 during the past 10 years but due to neighborhood problems, attendance has been down during the past year. The above listed figure was compiled by averaging the lowest and highest attendance during the reporting period. See chapter 7 for full information.

1

America's Largest Sunday School

AKRON BAPTIST TEMPLE, AKRON, OHIO

AKRON BAPTIST TEMPLE, Dr. Dallas Billington, Pastor and Founder

AKRON BAPTIST TEMPLE on a Sunday Morning

1

America's Largest Sunday School

AKRON BAPTIST TEMPLE, AKRON, OHIO

The Akron Baptist Temple began as a Bible study group in June 1934, when a young Baptist preacher, Dallas Billington, preached the Word of God to thirteen people in Rimer School, and an offering of $1.18 was collected. Today over six thousand attend Sunday School in the seven million dollar facilities of Akron Baptist Temple.

Billington was a lay Baptist preacher who worked in the Goodyear Tire and Rubber Company. One of his closest friends, J. Stanley Bond, was a dedicated, hard working Christian who worked in the warehouse.

The small congregation elected Bond as Sunday School superintendent. Modestly Stanley said he would do the best he could for a year, but at the end of the term he wanted to step aside and devote more time to singing in a religious quartet.

Young Dallas Billington saw in Bond the spark he knew was needed. "You stick with me, Stanley, and together we will build the biggest Sunday School in the world."

They did!

The two men most responsible for building the largest Sunday School in the world are Dr. Dallas Billington, minister, and a part time Sunday School superintendent, J. Stanley Bond.

Other churches frequently come to Bond to find out how they built the largest Sunday School. "Use this," says Bond, patting his Bible. "Believe it! You can't sell something you are not sold on yourself."

Bond believes that "almost any dedicated Christian can teach Sunday School." He goes on to say, "You must read your Bible and grow as a Christian. You must love people. If you love them, they'll know it and they will respond to what you teach them."

Bond has been Sunday School superintendent of Akron Baptist

15

Temple for thirty-four years. He sees his job of Sunday School superintendent as that of a business manager in an organization.

On Easter Sunday, 1935, less than a year after the first meeting, the church was formally organized with eighty members. Today the Akron Baptist Temple has over seventeen thousand members, and occupies an enormous six wing, seven million dollar complex at 2324 Manchester Road, Akron, Ohio. With an annual budget of over a million dollars, the church has organized over two hundred Baptist churches across America and overseas.

Dr. Billington gives the following reasons for the success of the Akron Baptist Temple.

1. *Godly Jealousy.* Dr. Billington indicates, "Godly jealousy is the secret of success at Akron Baptist Temple. I am jealous for souls and jealous for the reputation of God." One cannot talk with Dr. Billington without being impressed with his integrity and sincere love for Jesus Christ. When talking with unsaved people, Billington counts it a privilege to talk about Jesus Christ. When talking to a Christian, he counts it a challenge to motivate that person to live a more godly life.

"If a preacher is not jealous, he won't work, pray, or fight," stated Billington. He went on to say, "More words have been spent about love and less done about it. What ministers need is a little jealousy — for God."

Then with a twinkle in his eye, he said, "I'd jump down the throat of any preacher I'd catch visiting my sheep. I'm jealous for my people and I'm jealous for my work. I give no apologies. My work for Jesus Christ is the most important thing in my life." The enormous buildings of Akron Baptist Temple and the flow of crowds, encourages us to pray for more godly jealousy among the ministry today.

Further on the topic of "sheep stealing" Dr. Billington stated, "We don't steal sheep, but I think we steal a lot of goats. We *don't* go after members from other churches, but we go after souls — and a lot of unsaved church members are won to Jesus Christ."

2. *Evangelism and Visitation.* A newspaper man from the *Miami Herald* came to the Akron Baptist Temple seeking the "secret" of the work. During his Sunday morning visit, seven people asked him if he were a Christian. He later wrote that the "warm evangelism of the members and pastor of Akron Baptist Temple is its key to success."

The church has over five hundred laymen who go calling through the organized visitation program each week and make approximately eight hundred calls. The people are exhorted to go out two by two, which according to Billington is "God's plan for visitation." But in addition to the organized program of evangelism, the people take seriously the obligation of soul-winning in everyday life.

Billington feels the most effective visitation is made by the full time staff. The seven men on the staff make between sixty and seventy calls per week. Contrary to some of the other of the ten largest Sunday Schools, Billington would rather see quality than quantity in visitation. "I'd rather see five calls per week and see results, than fifty calls and no one attend our church." He added, "We don't race horses around the city, but we attempt to have an effective encounter with people."

When you read the book, *God Is Real,* an autobiography of Dallas Billington, you are impressed with the wave of souls that have been washed upon the shores of salvation through the ministry of Billington. One member stated, "Dr. Billington probably wins more souls to Christ per year than the sum total won by the average fundamentalistic Baptist church." Whether this is an exaggeration or not, there are thousands in the Akron Baptist Temple who look to Dallas Billington as their spiritual father.

3. *The Use of Sunday School Buildings.* The Akron Baptist Temple has a unique philosophy toward its facilities. Dr. Billington states, "We have never built a building, but that we needed it four years earlier." Billington's philosophy about Sunday School facilities is contrary to the laws of Sunday School growth that states, "You build a Sunday School room and the people will fill it." Dr. Billington is convinced that, "Sunday School pupils don't like to come to a large empty room." He goes on to say, "When Sunday School pupils come to a *crowd* and stand around on one another's feet and have to wait for a chair, they will come back to be where the action is. But pupils won't come to an empty classroom."

The church has a parking lot for over four thousand cars and room to expand. There are twenty-six doors to enter the building and surrounding the facilities are large enclosed hallways, called "malls" by Billington.

The unusual is used to attract the crowds. Recently an escalator was added so that the older folks driving in the parking lot would not have to walk up one flight of stairs to the main sanctuary. "The escalator is a first for a church," claims Billington.

4. *Promotion.* Another key to the success of Akron Baptist Temple is its multiple approach to promotion. Dr. Billington states, "We will use any promotional technique as long as it is godly and spiritual." To explain the above he stated, "Our aim is to win a soul, not false advertising. We will do anything possible to get people to attend, and present the gospel."

Reverend Charles Billington, son of the pastor, is active in Sunday School promotion. Many of the attendance building ideas have originated with him, since he came to be assistant pastor twenty-two years ago.

Over 100,000 pencils with the words, "Baptist Temple" have been given out. According to the senior Billington, no one will turn down a pencil. Also 100,000 pocket mirrors have been handed out with the phrase, "Home of the world's largest Sunday School." All these promotional techniques are to create momentum. "We want people to know that something is going on at our church," states Billington.

Placards are used on the local public bus line so that Billington boasts, "More people know where the Baptist Temple is than the county court house."

Lest the readers get a false impression of Akron Baptist Temple, there are seven major promotions per year. Billington feels that a major thrust every Sunday would lose its effectiveness. "Even though we have a number of promotional devices, we reach people through visitation and follow-up," stated Billington.

Even the church building itself helps in promotion. The tall building stands on a hill and can be seen ten miles away. Six foot tall red letters, B-A-P-T-I-S-T T-E-M-P-L-E, flash on and off so they may be seen from a distance. God has providentially placed the church so that six major highways cross within two miles of the church. The temple is one of the easiest spots in the city of Akron to reach.

Billington is convinced that we have to advertize the story of Jesus Christ just as the world advertizes pork and beans. And he quickly adds, "We should be more proud of Jesus than Madison Avenue is of its latest commercial."

When asked about his enthusiasm, Billington stated, "I'm still like a kid with a brand new red wagon. I'll talk about Jesus 'til He comes." To this Billington added that his favorite song is "Some Golden Daybreak, Jesus Will Come."

5. *Tithing.* Billington feels that tithing is one of the keys to the

success of God's work anywhere. To this he jokingly replies, "We only have one sermon on tithing — all year long."

Even though the church has seven millionaires, most of the money to meet the million dollar expenses per year comes from average folks. Billington believes they give more to God, "because when they get finished giving, they've got less to live on than the rich man."

Inflation doesn't worry Billington, for he believes that "the more people have, the more they will give." If a man is spiritually right with God and winning souls, money will be a minor matter.

Billington tells this story of financial problems when building his first building in 1937. Many of his people worked on WPA and the church could not secure a loan from the banks. Billington promised the people at Rimer School that God would help them build a church in Akron. Over the radio station he repeatedly said, "God will build a church for us." They began by putting in the concrete for the floors and the steel superstructure. Money did not come in, and they owed several thousand dollars. The church was asked to pay something on the material that had been used or there would be no material or work the following day. Of this Billington writes, "There would be no work in the temple: the hammers would not be ringing. Then we made up our minds, that since there would be no work the following day, we would meet all day for a prayer meeting." That night Billington went over to the half finished building, looked up through the superstructure and into the cold December evening. He writes, "It was cold and I shivered as I stood there pondering the things that had happened. I remember the disappointment when the industrialist had died, and we were denied help. All hope seemed gone. Every avenue of help seemed to be closed to us. Christmas would soon be here and there was little money in Akron for toys, let alone money for half finished churches." Billington had been accused of being, "overly enthusiastic" and not practical. He had been told that the depression days were not the time to build a church.

The contractor told him that only $5,000 was needed to finish the building. The next Sunday he announced the need for $5,000. He pleaded with every Christian who knew how to pray to ask God that this money be granted.

Monday morning after Billington left the hospital, calling on the sick, his wife informed him that an elderly lady had been trying to reach him. He drove to one of the better parts of Akron, went up on the porch and rang the doorbell. The lady who came to the door he describes as a "sweetheart grandmother." Billington went on to say, "Her hair was as white as snow, a silvery white." She had heard the broadcast. Having asked Dr. Billington to be seated, she left the room and went into the kitchen. Returning in a few minutes, she put a shoe box tied with calico strings before Dr. Billington. He described, "The box was so old it had begun to change color."

The lady stated, "Brother Billington, in this shoe box is $5,500. I heard your prayer for $5,000 to finish your building. Here is the money and $500.00 more. This is not a loan, but a gift."

Before Dr. Billington left, she kissed him on the forehead as if he had been her own son.

God answered prayer. A total of $8,200 came as a result of earnest intercession. Dr. Billington writes in his book that at the funeral of this unnamed saint who gave the money, "When I had her funeral service many years after our church was completed, people wondered about the preacher who wept; but I looked upon her then as my second mother, since my own mother was gone by that time and could not help me."

6. *Pastoral Leadership.* Dr. Billington is the leader of the church. He feels that God has called him to this position and his responsibility is a great one. He is chairman of the church board by virtue of the fact that he founded the church. When asked the question, "Do you have a finance committee?" Dr. Billington replied, "You're looking at him." This was not an ostentatious reply, simply a matter of fact that he is responsible for the raising and spending of the funds and serves as a business executive for a large company. But Dr. Billington is careful not to sign any checks and an audited statement is made each year of the total income and expenditure of the Akron Baptist Temple.

The congregation is the policy making body in the church, but Dr. Billington gives it leadership. The deacons are advisory in nature. Billington goes to the deacons to get their counsel and wisdom — but in the final analysis, he makes decisions based on the direction of congregational vote.

Some might feel that this is too much reponsibility for one man, especially a man of God who might be tempted with money. However, thirty-five years of ministry in the city of Akron has not brought the slightest murmur from any of his people that there has been wrong handling of so much as a penny of the church finances. Dr. Billington's integrity is motivation for his people to give more inasmuch as they know the money will be spent wisely in the service of God.

7. *Busing.* The Akron Baptist Temple was one of the first Sunday Schools in America to operate a busing program. Many years ago the church clientele was made up of the working class factory worker who could not afford an automobile. Many of these were Southerners and rode one of the forty Sunday School buses each Sunday. With the passing of time, the factory workers became more affluent, owning first one, then two automobiles. Their children were Ohio born and enjoyed the fruit of increasing wages.

Finally, Dr. Billington realized that Sunday School busing was too expensive. Many of the buses were rented from the public transit line and when the price went up from $30 to $40 per Sunday, he decided something had to be done.

A large promotion campaign was held and on a given Sunday, most of the buses were eliminated. That day there were more in Sunday School than the average. The people responded by driving or seeking public transportation. The church did not experience a dip in attendance.

Today, Akron Baptist Temple runs seven buses and brings in approximately 220 pupils per week. These are mostly children or old folks who have no transporation. Dr. Billington feels, "There's hardly any suburbanite who rides the bus today; they all have their cars." Akron Baptist Temple has changed with the times, shifting from a busing program to suburbanites who drive cars to be parked in the large paved lot. A staff of twenty-six men are needed to supervise the parking on a Sunday morning.

Also, the congregation has changed. No longer is Akron Baptist Temple made up of blue collar factory workers, or the hillbilly transplanted from West Virginia or Kentucky. Dr. Billington states in *God Is Real,* that one of the major purposes for beginning the Akron Baptist Temple was to provide a church with warm informal services and gospel preaching that Southerners in Akron could attend. He felt the ritual churches of Akron were cold and dead. But today the church clientele is different. When asked what class makes up the congregation, Billington replied, "All classes." There are indeed wealthy people in the church, but the clothes of some reflect the inner city ghetto. Over 250 young single adults attend the church. These are what society calls the "swingers," yet they are serious about the business of evangelism. The church is not tied to a neighborhood parish but draws from greater Akron.

8. *Separation from Worldly Influences.* Dr. Billington feels that a Christian should be separated from sinful influences that will damage his life. Says he, "A Sunday School teacher can't smoke, take part in dirty stories, go dancing. We want those who teach the Word of God to be clean." Also he feels that the church should not sponsor roller skating or swimming parties. At the Baptist Acres Camp owned by the church, the boys and girls swim at different periods, separated by half an hour.

However, Dr. Billington is not a rigid separationist. He prefers to emphasize the positive rather than the negative and tells the following story about his own son, Charles. One day he came home and found Charles sitting on the front stairs, crying. When Charles was asked why he was crying he said it was because all of the boys had gone to the picture show, left him alone and he couldn't go.

"Would you really like to go?" asked Dr. Billington.

"I'd give my life to go," replied the boy. "Why don't you go to shows, Dad?"

To this the father replied, "I'm a preacher. If I went I might keep somebody from heaven." The father explained to the son with all tenderness the lessons of being a stumbling block. But he went on to tell his son that there are some lessons in life he must learn for himself. He gave the boy a quarter and told him to go. Charles went several times, but the influence of Sunday School and the preaching of his Dad brought a crisis in his life. Charles later surrendered the picture show to the Lord, and today doesn't go.

Dr. Billington concluded, "You can't drive a kid; they have to be led." He went on further to say, "There is no freedom in Jesus Christ unless we have the freedom to choose."

The Future of Akron Baptist Temple

Even though Dr. Billington is sixty-six years old, he believes in the future of the church. Recently he wrote, "According to nature, sometime within the next thirty years I will be going home to be with God. It is my prayer that the next thirty years, should Jesus tarry, will find this church growing even more and winning even more souls for the Lord than it has in the past thirty years." Reverend Charles Billington, son of Dr. Dallas Billington, has been voted as successor to his father by the church. Because they see continual growth for Akron Baptist Temple, they plan to build a new auditorium that will seat 7,500. Because evening services do not draw the great crowds as the morning services, they want to divide the sanctuary according to the size of the crowd into two or three auditoriums so that each time there is a preaching service, the crowd fills the auditorium.

Dr. Billington sees TV as one of the means of getting the gospel to the unsaved. He states, "Color TV will draw people." At present, Dr. Billington's 10:00 A.M. adult class is televised live over the local ABC station WAKR. All of the engineers, announcers, and camera men are members of his church who donate their time to the telecast. However, the church has paid for their technical training. Dr. Billington feels the program will be nationwide in one to two years. He states, "We can reach more for Jesus through TV than any other means."

The Critics

Akron Baptist Temple is not without its critics. Some have complained that the adult Sunday School class in the auditorium doesn't have an accurate head count. The critics contend that Dr. Billington looks out on a Sunday morning in his class and makes an estimate. Billington counters this criticism by stating, "If we are off in our estimate, it is only by a hundred and there is no church close to us that would make a difference in the standing." Dr. Billington continued, "We take an actual count every two or three weeks. Each usher counts the three rows for which he is responsible for taking the offering. He writes the number on a slip of paper and these are all added by machine by the head usher."

On the Sunday this observer attended the church, Dr. Billington estimated that there were 2,200 in his class. The actual count by the ushers was 2,214. This observer counted 2,207 and feels that the count is as accurate as possible considering the large number of people to be tallied.

Another criticism of the Akron Baptist Temple, is that they put so much emphasis on evangelism that they minimize education. The critics are right in stating that the emphasis is evangelism, but they should not criticize the educational nature of the church without visiting and observing it in action. The quality of Bible teaching will compare favorably with any evangelical church in the country.

A new teacher is given the first volume of *Barnes' Notes on the Bible* and he may either purchase or with faithful attendance, receive the entire series free. Also, the new teacher is given a copy of *Handfuls of Purpose,* and those working in the children's division are given approximately $45.00 of flannelgraph material. This material is kept at the teacher's home, rather than at the church. Teacher's quarterly from Baptist Publications, Denver, Colorado, are used throughout the Sunday School except in the upper ages. However, no quarterlies are purchased for the pupil nor are teacher's manuals allowed in the classroom.

There are probably a thousand other factors attributing to the success of Akron Baptist Temple. These are the thousand workers who have joined Dr. Billington. Each would echo with Dr. Billington that the reason for success is God and His Word. For the Akron Baptist Temple gives high priority to the Bible. This success is reflected in Dr. Billington's oft quoted proverb, "I didn't write the Bible; I simply read it, preach it and teach it."

2

Empire of Evangelism

HIGHLAND PARK BAPTIST CHURCH,
CHATTANOOGA, TENNESSEE

HIGHLAND PARK BAPTIST CHURCH, Sunday Morning Service

2

Empire of Evangelism

HIGHLAND PARK BAPTIST CHURCH,
CHATTANOOGA, TENNESSEE

Highland Park Baptist Church is known as the *church of the green light*. The church stationery has a printed traffic signal with a green light and the word *GO*. Under the leadership of Dr. Lee Roberson, this church has taken seriously the words of Jesus, "*Go* ye into all the world and preach the gospel to every creature." This church is *going* in many ways: going through a daily half hour radio broadcast; going through *The Evangelist*, the weekly church paper with a circulation of 23,000; going through Camp Joy, a mission outreach project that gives free camping experience to more than three thousand each summer; going through a fleet of fifteen busses charged with visitation and evangelism of the greater Chattanooga area; going through forty-three mission outreach chapels; going through the Union Gospel Mission, a greater downtown mission for transient men; going through Tennessee Temple Elementary School, a first through eighth-grade church sponsored school with almost three hundred pupils enrolled; going through Tennessee Temple Schools, a Bible school, four year liberal arts college and three year seminary with a combined enrollment of almost two thousand; going through a world wide faith mission fund supporting approximately two hundred missionaries in both the home and foreign fields; and going through the extensive conference ministry of Dr. Lee Roberson who carries the message of Highland Park Baptist Church across the United States.

Highland Park Baptist Church occupied one building and sponsored one small chapel when Dr. Lee Roberson was called as pastor in 1942. Sunday School attendance averaged 470 and the church service ranged approximately 400 when Dr. Roberson began preaching. Today, the Highland Park Baptist Church maintains that it has the world's largest prayer meeting with a regular attendance of over 2,800, with larger audiences on special occasions.

Behind the empire of evangelism is the driving influence of Dr. Lee Roberson, who is affectionately called "Dr. Lee" by his friends. He was converted at age fourteen and preached his first sermon four years later. Dr. Roberson was educated in the University of Louisville and in the Southern Baptist Theological Seminary. He believes in the sanctity of work, having done various jobs from washing dishes to scrubbing floors to pay his way through school.

Dr. Roberson studied in Chicago under John Samples and was a noted singer over the Nashville and Louisville radio stations. After receiving offers in the field of music, Dr. Roberson rejected them because he felt "it was not the Lord's will."

As a young pastor, through personal Bible study, Dr. Roberson was led to accept the premillennial return of Christ. This transformed his ministry, giving him the urgency to win the lost for Christ.

Dr. Louis Entzminger, one of the pioneers of the 6-point record system used extensively in the Southern Baptist Sunday schools, had an impact on Highland Park Baptist Church. Dr. Entzminger held a Sunday School enlargement campaign in the Highland Park Baptist Church, at which time Arnold Chambers was converted. Many on the staff feel that Mr. Chambers was the second most influential person in the enlargement of the Highland Park Baptist Church. Dr. Roberson realizes that 90 per cent of those who come into the membership of the church, come through the Sunday School. He gives special attention to the Sunday School and considers it his most important evangelistic outreach.

He uses Wednesday night to instill a sense of loyalty and evangelistic passion into Sunday School teaching. Each teacher must pledge himself to faithful attendance at teachers' and officers' meetings, prayer meetings and Sunday services. Also, teachers must live consistent Christian lives. Once a year, the church asks them to re-affirm this pledge as they are installed for a new year of service.

Dr. Roberson meets with the bus pastors each Saturday morning. Each Sunday School bus has a driver and a pastor. The bus pastor's responsibility is evangelism, absentee follow-up, visitation and spiritual council to those who ride his bus.

Dr. Roberson not only exhorts others to visit; he does so himself.

At Sunday School rallies he indicates that when in town he makes up to ten calls per day. Nothing interferes with this except funerals and out of town engagements. On a number of occasions, Dr. Roberson has stated, "A home going pastor makes church going people."

The Wednesday evening teachers' and officers' meeting is one of the most important gatherings of the week. About 75 per cent of the 388 Sunday School teachers gather each Wednesday evening in the chapel next to the church auditorium. A report for each class and department is given and goals are assigned to challenge the people to reach more for Christ. The attendance of the forty-three church sponsored chapels is given. The promotion plans and coming special meetings are announced. Near the close of the meeting, pastor Roberson tries to fire each teacher with enthusiasm as one college teacher has said, "Challenging them to faithfulness and putting their best efforts to secure capacity attendance in the class for the next Sunday." Dr. Cliff Robinson, assistant pastor, teaches the Sunday School lesson to the teachers with suggested methods for presenting the class on Sunday morning. Dr. Roberson feels that, "If the Word of God is applied to the heart of the teacher with fire and enthusiasm, he in turn can become a better teacher on Sunday morning."

Dr. Robinson prepares an outline for the Sunday School lesson that is published weekly in the church newspaper, *The Evangelist.* This outline goes to all members and helps them prepare the Sunday School lesson. Dr. Robinson also distributes a mimeographed outline to the Sunday School teachers on Wednesday evening. This outline is three to five pages long and is a comprehensive commentary of Bible material. Some would criticize churches for writing their own Sunday School material, stating they would not have much quality; however, Dr. Robinson's mimeographed material for Sunday School would compare favorably with materials that are given to students in a Bible college book study class.

Promotion is important to Highland Park Baptist Church. A promotional leader is assigned for each month of the year with this person bearing the responsibility of carrying out a program of promotion. Every Sunday is a special day at Highland Park Baptist Church. Dr. J. R. Faulkner, co-pastor, says that the reasons for success are: "Blood, sweat and tears." He went on to say, "We have promotion in our Sunday School, but that doesn't keep people. You can get people through promotion, but keep them through a strong Bible teaching program." It takes hard work to run a good program according to Faulkner.

In 1969 Highland Park Baptist Church plans to contact all of the 322,000 people in the greater Chattanooga area with the gospel. A large computer type machine is placed at the front of the church. Each week the number of contacts that were made are added to the computer as a constant reminder of how many people have been reached for Christ.

Visitation is extremely important in the outreach of the church. Both absentees and lost people are visited. According to Lee Roberson, "We visit all our absent Sunday School students every week." In addition to this, lost people are visited. People are asked for the names of unchurched neighbors or friends. These are added to the prospect list and are then visited.

People go out two by two on Thursday evenings. Before sending his workers out visiting, Dr. Roberson reminds the workers that those being dealt with during the week are expected to come forward in the church service on Sunday either for salvation or church membership. This, states Dr. Roberson, brings all members to the Lord's day with keen anticipation, looking forward to "the fruit of the harvest."

The secretary of the Sunday School gleans the rolls to get visitation prospects. These prospects and absentees are in turn channeled to the superintendent and then to the Sunday School teacher for the actual visit. When a worker arrives on visitation night, he receives a card according to the geographical location of the city. Absentees are assigned; unsaved prospects are not. But workers are encouraged to take the cards of the unsaved and make a contact for the gospel.

The week this observer was at the church, 290 came to the Thursday night visitation supper and approximately forty came in after the supper to go out on the visitation program. Some took five cards, others took one, a few took none.

Even teenagers get involved in the visitation program of Highland Park Baptist Church. Sixty teenagers were involved on the week mentioned. After the visit, the teens go to a home for recreation and fellowship. Dr. Roberson indicated, "Work first; socialize second."

In addition, phone calls, cards, and letters are sent out to contact the unsaved. According to Faulkner, "Thousands of letters are sent out each week to members and contacts." On the week this observer visited the church, over five thousand contacts were made.

Highland Park Baptist Church has no Board of Christian Education. Sunday School policy is voted on by the congregation as a whole. "This is a congregational government and the people are responsible for their Sunday School," stated Dr. Roberson.

The church has no unified budget, but all money given through the Sunday School goes to the church treasury. The budget and finance committees are responsible for the spending of the money.

Highland Park Baptist Church believes in the old fashioned evangelistic meeting. For the past eighteen years the following evangelistic cycle has been held: the mid-winter revival, the Bible conference in April, the summer Bible conference in July, and the missionary conference in November. Unsaved people are invited to walk down the aisle and accept Jesus Christ as Saviour. Dr. Roberson indicated that approximately twenty-three people accept Christ each Lord's day at Highland Park Baptist Church. In the past twenty-seven years, there has only been one service when no one responded.

The Highland Park Baptist Church led the Southern Baptist Convention in baptisms, the last seven years it was a member. According to Dr. Roberson, Highland Park Baptist Church never left the Southern Baptist Convention, but the Convention stopped listing them in the yearbook. But one year after Highland Park Baptist Church was dropped from the Southern Baptist rolls, executives from the association asked to have the baptisms of Dr. Roberson listed in their yearbook.

At a recent Sunday morning service at which J. R. Faulkner was preparing people for revival, he stated, "We need the white heat of revival. . . . I want each person in this room to hear this revival speaker." Cottage prayer meetings are held for revival. Faulkner stated, "I believe that as a collective force, the prayer meetings can call on God to rend the heavens, to send revival and to shake the city of Chattanooga."

As one walks in the front door of the sanctuary, he is greeted with the sign, "The World's Most Visited Church." A large map with pins indicate visitors have come from almost every section of the United States to Chattanooga, Tennessee. On the church bulletin one reads, "Every visitor, an honored guest." During the service, visitors are asked to stand and they are given an envelope. A statement on the envelope says the visitor's offering will go to foreign missions. This way, Dr. Roberson believes he can encourage visitors to give to the work of the Lord, yet not ask money for the local church from those who are the honored guests of the church.

As one sits in the service, he immediately realizes that the preaching is understandable. The sermon is in everyday language, and the personal touch reaches over the pulpit to the hearts of those who are listening. But the sermons are not mere emotionalism; "knowledge on fire" characterizes the preaching of Highland Park Baptist Church. There is no shouting or poor taste in emotionalism; just the warmth of the moving of the Spirit of God.

This observer saw seven adults go forward on Sunday morning. A core of men and women efficiently dealt with each person who responded to the invitation. They knelt and prayed the prayer of repentance. Afterwards, Dr. Roberson challenged each one from the pulpit. He asked them three questions. (1) Do you believe that Jesus died on the cross to save sinners? Each person responded, "yes." (2) Are you trusting Jesus as your personal Saviour? Once again, they said, "yes." And finally, (3) do you want to follow the Lord in baptism and live for Him? Those who came forward were baptized that morning. There were no children who came forward on this Sunday morning.

Once a person is converted, and a member of Highland Park Baptist Church, much is expected of him. In a printed statement of what is expected of the members of Highland Park Baptist Church, the following statement of purpose is given. (1) *Attendance*. Every member is expected to be in attendance on Sunday morning, Sunday evening, and Wednesday prayer meeting. (2) *Read the Bible*. Every Christian is expected to read God's Word so they may grow in grace. (3) *Talk to God in prayer*. Not only are they exhorted to pray, but they are given suggestions as to what things they should pray for. (4) *Talk to someone about God each day*. This way, each person in expected to win souls and as Andrew brought his brother, Simon Peter, so each person should bring their friends and relatives to Christ. (5) *Give*. Each person is supposed to be a tither.

One of the criticisms of Dr. Lee Roberson at Highland Park Baptist Church is the fact that they add their mission chapels in their Sunday School attendance. Some feel the chapels should not be listed, nor should Highland Park Baptist Church be listed second in the survey because their Sunday School attendance is not at one geographic location. When faced with the question, Dr. Roberson gave the following answers:

1. These chapels have never supported themselves. If we were to cut them off and make them local missions, they would have to give up for financial reasons. The mother church underwrites them financially, supplies musical programs, and supplies preachers from Tennessee Temple Schools. Many of the chapel buildings have been purchased by the Highland Park Baptist Church and if the local congregation, which is usually in a very poor area, had to pay for the building, the work would never have begun.

2. If a church is able to support itself full time, it will be cut off and become indigenous. Since Dr. Roberson has come to Highland Park Baptist Church, thirteen chapels have become self-supporting churches and are not now counted in the Sunday School attendance.

3. Dr. Faulkner indicated, "We could drive these people to our main location in our Sunday School buses, but feel folks should worship God in their own neighborhood. We are not out for larger numbers at our main location, but to reach people the best way possible."

4. Finally, Dr. Roberson indicated that they want to keep the church as a unit. This includes the Union Gospel Mission, Camp Joy, the 199 missionaries, plus the 43 chapels. For these reasons, they count them in the total attendance. For those who are skeptics, they will have to evaluate the four reasons and draw conclusions for themselves.

Dr. Roberson was asked the source of finances to support the broad outreach of the church. "Tithing is the secret," indicated Dr. Roberson. The church does not make pledges but emphasizes that every member should be a tither. Dr. Roberson requires the seventy deacons and eighty ushers to tithe. He went on to state that 75 per cent of the members are tithing.

Dr. Roberson's demand for lay leadership in the local church has led to many facets of the church's total program. Out of the need for trained lay leadership was born Tennessee Temple Schools. When seeking lay workers to fill church offices Dr. Roberson was often faced with those who were willing to work but felt unqualified to fill these vacancies. A church sponsored night school including Bible study, English, music and speech was begun. On July 3, 1946, the church voted to turn the night school idea into a church sponsored junior college and Bible school with Dr. Roberson as president. Today, the fifty-five buildings of Tennessee Temple Schools are a monument to the ongoing quality and the outreach of the gospel. The multi-million dollar school, even though not accredited, has college recognition for training of public school teachers.

Dr. Roberson's office reminds you of his heart — foreign missions and preaching. One wall of his office is covered with a map of the world which reflects the passion he has for foreign missions. The book cases are covered with curios and missionary memorabilia that constantly reminds him to get the gospel out to every creature. The other material in his office are notebooks filled with sermons. These remind you that Dr. Roberson is first and primarily a preacher of the Word of God.

Even though the church was begun in 1890 and had a membership of 1,000 when Dr. Roberson came, it is easy to see that he has given the impetus and drive to the vast outreach that has made Highland Park Baptist Church an empire of evangelism.

3

A Great Sunday School

THE FIRST BAPTIST CHURCH, DALLAS, TEXAS

FIRST BAPTIST CHURCH, Dallas, Texas

3

A Great Sunday School

THE FIRST BAPTIST CHURCH, DALLAS, TEXAS

The history of First Baptist Church, Dallas, Texas, is the story of two great men of God, Dr. George W. Truett and Dr. W. A. Criswell. The 20th century has only seen two pastors of this great church. George W. Truett took the pastorate in 1897 and continued until his death in 1944, then Dr. Criswell became pastor for the next twenty-five years. When the transition between these two outstanding men took place, Sunday School enrollment stood at 3,940, average attendance at only 1,000. First Baptist Church was not known for its Sunday School but rather the great preaching of Dr. Truett.

Wally Amos Criswell was called to the pastorate of First Baptist Church, not so much for his widely known reputation, but for his his dynamic preaching. When newspaper reporters were given the story of the new pastor, one stuttered, "Do you mean the great First Baptist Church is calling a young unknown to succeed Dr. Truett?" Perhaps the same question was in many minds throughout the church and city. The church had just come through the great Truett era, not realizing that a greater Criswell era was to dawn upon them.

Dr. Criswell did not try to mimic Truett but brought his own personal dynamism to the pulpit. He stated, "I can't be like Dr. Truett, much as I would like to be." Dr. Criswell went on to say, "I preach like a holy roller; I know it and can't help it. I have always spoken vigorously. I know that is a weakness. I have all my heart and soul in the ministry and the gospel. I am not proud that I sometimes shout and my voice cracks. I just get so interested and excited that I just can't help it."[1]

---

[1]Leon McBeth, *The First Baptist Church of Dallas* (Grand Rapids: Zondervan Publishing House, 1968), p. 105.

In addition to preaching, Criswell built a great Sunday School and many consider it the greatest Sunday School in America because of the commitment of laymen to teaching the Word of God, because of the closely graded program, because of steady growth, because of a solid educational philosophy and because of the numbers that have been brought to Christ. The First Baptist Church has an annual budget that is double the amount given by churches with the same size Sunday School. Also, it has twice as much Sunday School floor space as other equal size Sunday Schools.

Two individuals assisted Dr. Criswell in the beginning of making the Sunday School great. Dr. W. L. Howse, then professor of Religious Education at Southwestern Baptist Theological Seminary in Ft. Worth served as interim Director of Christian Education beginning in June of 1946. Howse, considered one of the nation's leading Sunday School authorities, began reorganizing the Sunday School and laid the foundation for the attendance advance that was to come later. Howse practiced at First Baptist Church what he often taught in seminary classrooms, that the key to Sunday School growth is through teacher training. These trained teachers provided Sunday School growth in the next decade.

A year later, W. H. Souther came to First Baptist Church as Minister of Music and Education. He not only up-graded and modified the music program, but he moved the Sunday School from a departmentally-graded basis to an age-graded basis and integrated the program into an overall church outreach. Criswell said of Souther, "He was the guiding genius of the Sunday School program as we know it."[2]

One of the problems facing Souther was the reorganization and enlargement of the adult classes in the church. At that time, the adult classes were like many of those presently operating in many of the ten largest Sunday Schools. At First Baptist Church, the large semi-independent Bible classes were organized without regard to age. The church had little oversight of these classes, because they elected their own teachers, received and dispersed their own funds, and some of them met at other places in downtown Dallas removed from the church building. One class conducted a radio Bible class, another class gave as much as $10,000 a year to missions at Christmas time. McBeth in his book, *The First Baptist Church of Dallas*, tells some of the problems Criswell and

Souther had with the large independent Bible classes. The church could not elect successors, yet the church's reputation was at stake when poor teaching continued. Apparently, one of the poorer teachers was receiving a monthly stipend of $34.00. The deacons voted to increase this to $50.00 if the teacher would stop teaching![3]

The present Minister of Evangelism, Dr. James Bryant, indicates that the large independent classes are still in existence in the church, and are accomplishing much for the ministry of the Word of God. However, he indicated the large classes have been integrated into the local program. While most of the new prospects and additions are directed into the closely graded adult classes some are enrolled in the independent classes. However, Bryant believes the key to overall Sunday School growth is the closely graded program. He stated, "We must closely grade our classes and when they grow, divide them for continued growth."

Criswell and Bryant are presently committed to the grading system for adults. They feel age grading of adults will produce better teaching which in turn will result in stronger Christians.

The closely graded Sunday School classes of adults could never have been accomplished without new buildings and facilities. (The First Baptist Church has approximately twice as much educational floor space as the other churches in this study of the same attendance and is seeking to build or buy space enough to double their present educational floor space. The other churches have a large Sunday School class meeting in the sanctuary and all of the adults who attend are counted in the attendance roll.) However, First Baptist Church of Dallas has a large number of adults in small rooms for group discussion and study in the Word of God. Age grading of adults not only means more workers must become involved, but more money must be spent on curriculum and more capital invested in facilities.

In addition to the few large independent Bible classes and the many age-graded classes, the church has some classes graded by occupation and interest as well. There is a special class for medical and dental personnel and students. There are special classes for the oral deaf, silent friends, and special education for those with mental deficiencies, as well as classes for Chinese and Japanese in

---

[3]P. 255.

their native languages. Plans are being made for adding a class for professional athletes and a class for airline stewardesses.

Bryant indicates another purpose for closely grading is, "responsibility purpose." By this he means a vast number of adult laymen must accept the *responsibility* for the Sunday School and *purpose* to cause the attendance to grow. Every prospect becomes some teacher's personal responsibility.

When Dr. Criswell first came the congregation was made up of many middle aged teachers and older folks. A massive drive was put on to attract young couples to the downtown church. Dr. Criswell began to reach young couples with children as he emphasized the nursery as the "hand shake" of the church. Young couples responded and chiefly made up the large influx of people during early 1950. The very fact that so many have stayed with the church for the past fifteen years reflects the total ministry of First Baptist Church to its people. The largest group joining the church week by week is still composed of young families.

There is a definite philosophy concerning the use of buildings at the First Baptist Church. Buildings cannot reach people; organized people reach people. On the other hand, a Sunday School cannot enlarge without space. A church cannot add additional classes and departments without additional space. The present plan of Sunday School outreach places a priority on expanding Sunday School floor space for an expanded organization and consequently an expanded attendance. Bryant indicated, "A church can't grow in its auditorium but can expand through its Sunday School." In analyzing his attendance, Bryant stated, "We have slowed down and will go down unless we enlarge our educational facilities."

The first Baptist Church is committed to staying downtown. It owns two large parking garages of five stories each located four blocks from the heart of the city. The church's property is valued at eight million dollars and is considered on the "cutting edge of the downtown area."

The church has optimistic plans for the future with still another parking building with education space on the drawing board costing 3-4 million dollars. Seven floors could be added to the already existing Truett building for about 2 million dollars. Also, a 2-3 million dollar dining building with office facilities and educational space is planned. One of the buildings presently owned by the First Baptist Church is the activities building with a collegiate size gym and bleachers, a gymnastic room, a four lane bowling alley with automatic pin spotters, a large skating rink, and a game room.

The church has a definite philosophy of recreation. Since the human body is the temple of the Holy Spirit, the church must minister to the whole man. The recreational facilities are used during the day, for pre-school education classes and activities for housewives, at noon by downtown businessmen, followed by a full organized program in the evenings and on Saturday. Every available nook and cranny in the activity building is utilized on Sunday morning for Sunday School classes. Some classes meet in the snack bar, bowling alley and gymnastic room.

Evangelism has been one of the basic steps in the growth for church and Sunday School alike. In Criswell's earlier years, revivals were common place, some of them lasting four weeks. At least one revival is still held annually. Dr. Criswell still believes in giving an invitation Sunday mornings and evenings, as well as Wednesday evenings. He preaches for decisions. The term evangelism has a specific meaning to First Baptist Church. Evangelism is getting people to Christ, getting people baptized, and getting Christians into the total life of the church. The great commission is not completed without a person's involvement in Christian service.

The church staff is united around evangelism, not Christian education as might be suspected by many. There are twelve full time Christian education directors, but they are responsible to Dr. James Bryant, Minister of Evangelism. He coordinates the educational program around evangelism. Each of the Directors of Christian Education has the full-time responsibility of supervising the educational work in one Sunday School division. The divisions are: Cradle Roll, Nursery, Beginner, Primary, Junior, Junior High, Senior High, College and Career, Business and Professional (or Single Adults), Young Adults, Median Adults, and Adults.

Monday night is visitation night and the church has an organized program of outreach. Approximately one hundred to three hundred will attend the organized program, but Bryant reports, "Some don't participate on Monday evening, but do make the calls that are assigned to them." He states that approximately 1,200 reported home visits are made each week from the First Baptist Church. If Dallas homes contain family members equal to the national average, this means approximately 5,400 individual family members are touched for Christ, by the church, each week.

A recent program of evangelism reflects the changing program of First Baptist Church to become relevant to the needs of Dallas. One weekend a census was taken by telephone of forty thousand homes. More than seven hundred laymen from the church were involved. The purpose of the census was to determine if a family is unchurched. (A family was considered unchurched if it did not attend its church at least once a month.) Approximately four thousand families were found to be unchurched. Each of these families began to receive letters monthly from Dr. Criswell urging church attendance. In addition to this direct-mail campaign, a three night Personal Evangelism Institute was held to train people in sowing, cultivating, and harvesting. Fifteen hundred attended. Each team of two trained personal evangelists was then assigned four families to reach.

Each team was given the following instructions, "Go and make a personal contact and (1) give your testimony of how you received Christ. (2) Present them with a gift of the Gospel of John. (3) Determine if the family is reachable by our Sunday School." This was called a family to family campaign. Each family was instructed to invite one of the prospect families into their homes, thus showing interest in them as friends. Next, the man was to invite the man of the house to a luncheon held in a downtown restaurant where Christian men gave their testimonies. Bryant feels the church must "positionize" men as Christians in the business community by witnessing for Christ. Ladies planned neighborhood luncheons for witnessing to ladies. Teenagers planned parties at which they witnessed to their unsaved friends.

The church bought a block of tickets to see the Dallas Chapparells of the American Basketball Association and made it "First Baptist Night." Professional athletes who attend the church are used to giving their testimonies to attract men to the church. Bryant feels, "If a man has gone out four or five times with a member of our church and enjoyed himself in the presence of Christians, he will be more likely to attend our spring revival at the church."

In addition to this evangelistic outreach, Bryant is organizing a *Fisherman's Club* of six hundred men who will be divided into teams of four to honeycomb Dallas with neighborhood witnessing teams. These men will be trained in evangelism and can make Christianity relevant to others around them. Out of this group will come a "task force" of one hundred men to reach out into the world once a year in a layman's witnessing tour. Plans now include an evangelistic thrust in Mexico City in 1969 and Tokyo in 1970. Dr. Criswell and the two hundred voice Chapel Choir (teens) will accompany the men.

The power of the layman at work is necessary, but the culmination of the outreach of First Baptist Church comes on Sunday when Dr. Criswell preaches the Word of God. The warmth of his invitation attracts many prospective members to move their church letters, as well as those seeking Christ. They are all asked to walk forward during the singing of the invitational hymn. After the invitation, Criswell smiles broadly, lifts his arms and states, "This is the Lord's harvest" pointing to those who have come forward. It can still be said of Dr. Criswell, his greatest joy is seeing lost people come to Jesus Christ.

The church is in the process of computerizing its membership in order to keep in more personal touch with its 15,000 members. The city of Dallas is divided into two mile square sections. Teams of personal evangelists will be assigned to these sections of the city. It is their responsibility to telephone, visit and follow-up those within their section. Every newcomer to Dallas should receive a witness from some Christian living near by. The key to this approach is, "A man where he is — witnessing for Christ."

Sunday School enrollment is important to the First Baptist Church. Some of the other churches in the study do not keep enrollment figures. A present goal of the church is by April 1970 to enroll the census. According to Bryant, "Enrollment is more important than attendance." He went on to explain that if attendance went up but the people were not enrolled, the new contacts might not return. However, if people are committed to the Sunday School by enrollment, attendance will automatically rise. Dr. Criswell's philosophy follows this line, "If you can show a trend, you're doing alright." In the appendix of the book, *The First Baptist Church of Dallas*, Sunday School enrollment figures are listed rather than average attendance figures. The figures indicate that there has been a steady enrollment growth through the years. When Dr. Criswell came to the church in 1944, there were 3,940 enrolled with about 1,000 attending. Today there are 8,655 enrolled with an average attendance of 4,500.

The annual Palace Theater Services, on the week before Easter, at noon, Monday through Friday, are held in the downtown Palace Theater. For fifty-three consecutive years the church has had this outreach. Nearly two thousand attend daily, 80 per cent of whom are not members of the First Baptist Church. Only Dr. Truett and Dr. Criswell have preached these services.

The Critics

The First Baptist Church has been criticized for segregation against the people from the inner city. The main church service is held in the sanctuary with Dr. Criswell preaching. However, in an adjoining hall used for large weddings and funerals, a smaller church called the Good Shepherd Department meets with 200 to 220 and a staff member assigned to that group does the preaching. However, Bryant answers the charge, "They [the people from the economically poor section of Dallas] won't come over to the main service." He went on to indicate, "They were welcomed and encouraged to come but they felt more at home in their own service."

There are six buses tied to this Good Shepherd work which transport people on Sunday morning. Bryant indicated, "Affluent people won't ride Sunday School buses." He went on to state that the church no longer tries to bring folks in from the suburbs through Sunday School busing. The buses are sent only to low-rent housing projects.

A second criticism is that First Baptist Church counts its six missions in its total attendance records. The mission Sunday Schools at these outlying locations have approximately five hundred to six hundred in attendance. Thirteen Sunday School buses go out from the downtown church and transport people to these missions, two of which meet in the downtown facility, and four of which are located in West Dallas. They are not economically self-supporting, being located in economically deprived neighborhoods. The Director of the Missions Ministry sits in on the cabinet meeting of the staff at the downtown church. Each mission has a full time pastor, associate, and secretary. Many laymen work in these missions. One mission is conducted in Spanish, another in sign language, and the other four in English.

The third criticism of First Baptist Church is that people get lost in such a large organization. This is not true. First of all, every new member is discussed by name at a bi-monthly staff meeting. An attempt is made to involve every new member in some part of the church program. A recent new member stated, "I didn't think a church this large could be so interested in me as an individual." Bryant feels that First Baptist Church can better meet the spiritual needs of an individual than a suburban church because they have so many ministries. First Baptist members who are hospitalized usually get more attention from staff and laity of the First Baptist Church than members of smaller churches would.

Pastoral Leadership

For forty-seven years Dr. Truett led the church. It is said of him, "He didn't build on himself, but on Jesus Christ." Dr. Criswell has followed that heritage. As one thoroughly examines the book, *The First Baptist Church of Dallas* one is convinced that Dr. Criswell is not a dictator nor a despot. The congregation is still the final seat of authority at First Baptist Church. However, with the enormous membership of the church (nearly 15,000) the 236 deacons are in effect the policy setting board of the church. Of them McBeth writes, "The deacons have full confidence in the pastor and regards this confidence justified by his unerring leadership. In recent years they have never failed to go along with Criswell's major proposals."[4] But Dr. Criswell has repeatedly said that he prefers preaching and shepherding the flock to the business and administrative work of the church.

Bryant indicates, "The staff belongs to the pastor." He indicated that the pastor was responsible for hiring, although the personnel committee of the deacons approved each new employee. Criswell's leadership begins with his staff and works out to his people. He is the great motivator of the church, moving people to give, work and be faithful to the work of God.

The work of First Baptist Church is built on the staff rather than the single personality of Dr. Criswell. Even though Criswell gives leadership, the church is not built on his personality. One person made the comment, "If Dr. Criswell were to die, the church would go on because the men of the church plan to reach the city of Dallas for Christ."

When you listen to Dr. Criswell, you are aware of his erudite scholarship and the Ph.D. is more than a plaque to hang on the wall. At the same time, you are aware of his convictions. His latest book, *Why I Preach the Bible Is Literally True*, indicates a firm stand for the Word of God. In 1959, he attacked biological evolution and in 1960 he opposed the election of a Roman Catholic

---

[4]P. 334.

as President of the United States. He has continued to attack the liquor traffic and has made such statements as, "No Baptist should have beer in his refrigerator."

The 11:00 A. M. church service is televised live over a five state area. Billy Graham, a member of the church, is urging the church to expand its television ministry on a nation-wide basis. All three services each Sunday are broadcast over radio. Some people drive thirty to forty miles to church, primarily because they love to hear Dr. Criswell preach. Bryant indicated, "They get something here they don't get elsewhere." He indicated that Christ is faithfully preached through an expository ministry whereby the layman can become intellectually, emotionally, and volitionally involved.

The key to the growth and outreach of the First Baptist Church in the past twenty-five years has been Wally Amos Criswell. When he first came to the church, he did not rest on the laurels of Truett. He began to build. He challenged the people to greater faith in God. "We will go on and up with our various works. We will give more money to missions than ever before. We will have five thousand in Sunday School every Sunday. We will win more people to Christ. We will build up and out for the glory of God." His vision has come true.

4

The Fastest Growing Sunday School

FIRST BAPTIST CHURCH, HAMMOND, INDIANA

FIRST BAPTIST CHURCH, Hammond, Indiana, on a Sunday Morning

4

The Fastest Growing Sunday School

FIRST BAPTIST CHURCH, HAMMOND, INDIANA

Hammond is located in the flat lands at the foot of Lake Michigan where water stands in the ditches and the soot from industry settles on the buildings. This is not a very likely place to build a large Sunday School according to the popular idea that Christianity prospers in the suburbs. But, First Baptist Church of this city has the fastest growing Sunday School in America.

When the author approached the city of Hammond, he pulled into an oil packed driveway of a service station to ask the attendant how to find the First Baptist Church. A beer bellied man in an old fashioned undershirt, spit tobacco juice in a dirty box and said, "Follow the blue buses. That church must have a million of 'em."

Within a few minutes, a blue bus came by and we followed it to the downtown, inner city area of Hammond.

Two boys came across the railway tracks, jumped across the puddles left by melting snow in the unpaved alley. Their shoes were scuffed and their pants were unpressed, but with Bibles in hand they headed to Sunday School. Next, a Cadillac drove up and a lady in a fashionable tailored coat and stylish boots stepped out into the snow. She too was going to Sunday School.

The Sunday School of First Baptist Church, Hammond, Indiana, is not filled with little shriveled old ladies, but young families, sophisticated young single adults, soldiers, and the poor right out of the tenement houses. All attend a dynamic growing Sunday School with a massive outreach.

First Baptist Church averaged 3,978 in attendance this past year, up from 3,342 in attendance the previous year. On one Sunday in March 1969 there were over 6,100 in attendance. When Dr. Jack Hyles came as pastor ten years ago the Sunday School was averaging over 700. Because of these overwhelming figures for expansion, the church has the fastest growing Sunday School in America.

During the Sunday School hour, special education classes are conducted to reach approximately seventy mentally retarded children. There are three Sunday School classes for the deaf, reaching another forty-five pupils. Two Spanish Sunday School classes are taught for those who do not understand the English tongue. They may also remain for church and hear the Word of God in their own language.

The Hammond City Rescue Mission sponsored by the First Baptist Church reaches the transient in downtown Hammond. A clothing closet is made available to any family having need of clothing. The church also provides a barbershop for the indigent who need this service. In addition, there is a Sunday afternoon Bible class in which underprivileged children from the neighborhood may come and receive a hot lunch, then hear the Word of God. These children are not bused to the church since they are within walking distance of the church.

Also, the church has an outreach through Hyles Publications, a ministry to distribute books, pamphlets, tapes and records.

Reasons for Growth

When Hyles was asked the reasons for the success of his Sunday School, he listed the following:

1. *Simplification of Organization.* The main reason for the success of First Baptist Church is the simple approach to organization and administration. Hyles believes that the administration of the average church is in the hands of too many people. For instance, he feels that the church should not have a music committee to tell the director of music how to run his program. Rather, he believes in giving a job to a man and letting the man perform the function. If the appointed person is not satisfactory, the church should employ someone else. He believes that many laymen are so busy doing secondary things that they do not have time for soul winning.

2. *Soul Winning Evangelism.* The whole program of First Baptist Church is geared to evangelistic outreach. But this church does not have a single approach. Rather, the term *multiple approach* could characterize the outreach.

Dr. Hyles tells the story of going fishing as a boy and bringing home one fish. Later, he saw a man fishing with two lines, catching twice as many fish. A little later, he saw a man with a snare line, with many hooks, of course, bringing in many fish. As a result of this experience, Hyles indicated he would not fish for men with one hook, but rather many hooks. Hyles feels the church should employ as many techniques of outreach as possible to win as many people as possible.

3. *Training Laymen to Do What the Preacher Does.* Dr. Hyles believes the main task of the pastor is winning souls. He has a reputation for being among people presenting Jesus Christ. According to Hyles, First Baptist Church has hundreds of people who are able and do win souls every year. He teaches that every Christian can be a soul winner and has not fulfilled his duty to God when he sits on a church committee. The only way to fulfill one's duty is to be active in evangelism.

4. *The Leadership of the Pastor.* The spiritual program of First Baptist Church is planned by the pastor. Hyles stated, "If we have a visiting speaker, I choose him. If we have a Sunday School drive, I plan it and present it."

The business of the church is actually completed in congregational meetings, for they are the seat of authority in the local church. The board of deacons is not a policy making body, but can only recommend policy and decisions to the church. The deacons constitute an advisory board, and as such work with the pastor. The pastor always confides in his deacons before carrying a recommendation to the church business meeting. However, in First Baptist Church the board has such confidence in the pastor that they rarely fail to reinforce his recommendation to the congregation. And the church has such confidence in the pastor and the board that it rarely turns down their requests. Hyles states, "We only have pastor, deacons and people, which is the New Testament plan — very simple."

5. *Sunday School Busing.* The First Baptist Church has sixty-five Sunday School buses and brings in 1,800 pupils through this outreach. Hyles does not call Sunday School busing a principle, but the outgrowth of a program of evangelism. He is aware of those who criticize his busing program and points to his previous pastorate, Miller Road Baptist Church in Garland, Texas, where he had comparable growth to the Hammond Church, but did not have a single Sunday School bus.

Hyles stated, "The principle is to reach everybody in every way possible, and since First Baptist Church is a downtown church there is the need to provide transportation." So he naturally went to a busing ministry.

At present some of the buses travel as far away as the Great Lakes Naval Training Center, some 80 miles north of Chicago. This involves an hour and a half one way trip. Also, a bus brings students from the Moody Bible Institute in downtown Chicago. Those who ride these buses are provided "chicken in a basket" from a commercial restaurant to eat on the ride home.

Hyles meets with his bus workers a 9:00 o'clock on Wednesday evening after prayer meeting. There are usually 150 drivers and bus captains present. The drivers are responsible for the navigation of the routes and care of the equipment. Each bus has a captain responsible for visitation, absentee follow up and spiritual care of those who ride the bus. The captain is responsible for filling the bus with students. In addition, there are approximately twenty-five men and boys who are responsible for parking the buses. According to Hyles, "It's a big job to park these buses." Hyles plans to add about twelve buses a year for expansion in the future.

6. *Informal Type of Service.* The services of First Baptist Church are well planned but are not ritualistic. The basis is reaching the common man for Jesus Christ. Hyles believes that the common man wants both a message and a church to identify with. In his preaching he uses a lot of illustrations which might be called "homey." Hyles went on to state, "I believe that the average pulpit is above the people's heads. There is profundity in simplicity." He practices this principle by keeping his sermons on the level of the average man.

Dr. Hyles feels that the Book of Acts is the standard by which the church should be organized today. Because of this, he confesses to reading three books in the Bible every day, Psalms, Proverbs and the Book of Acts.

Because of the simplicity of worship and function, Dr. Hyles believes that the First Baptist Church of Hammond, Indiana, is akin to the New Testament church. And with the simplicity, he feels that the preaching of the gospel is central to his service.

7. *Writing Their Own Sunday School Literature.* Dr. Jack Hyles feels a publishing house does not know the needs of his church well enough to plan curriculum. He stated, "When a man is sick he

doesn't take the next bottle off the shelf; rather, he takes the medicine he needs. So also when a child is growing up, he doesn't take the next lesson in the quarterly but rather, he takes the material he needs to grow." Hyles feels that the Sunday School literature representing the evangelical market is good material, but he'd rather write his own. He went on to suggest, "Sunday School literature is only as good as the teacher who sits in the classroom."

You must examine the Sunday School literature to understand his teacher's meeting every Wednesday evening. At 6:00 p.m. on Wednesday evening the teachers and officers meet together for an evening meal. Beginning at 6:30, the actual meeting is divided into three twenty minute sections.

During the first twenty minutes, Dr. Hyles seeks to motivate the people. He urges his teachers to visit, he explains the goals or contests that are scheduled, and encourages them to faithfulness. This is a time for enthusiasm. At this time announcements are made, reports are given and prizes are awarded.

During the second twenty minutes, Dr. Hyles teaches the lesson to the Sunday School teachers. All pupils in the Sunday School study the same lesson. The large percentage of Sunday School teachers who attend indicates they are getting enough help to merit their time. Many express the opinion that Dr. Hyles is the best teacher in the church.

For the third twenty minutes, the classes divide for meetings with departmental sessions. Different members of the staff apply the lesson to the specific age levels. Teachers are given aids and helps for next Sunday's instruction. Each teacher receives a mimeographed lesson outline to help in his individual lesson preparation. Hyles believed that if the Word of God is applied to the heart of the teacher, then the layman can walk into the classroom with heart aflame and apply the lesson to his class.

Only men teach boys once students reach the first grade in the Sunday School of the First Baptist Church. Use of male teachers grew out of conviction. The church feels that the teacher should be an example and that boys will look up to a Christian man and will follow his example.

8. *Second Sunday School.* One of the unique innovations of the First Baptist Church is the second Sunday School. The Sunday School facilities were so overcrowded, there was no room to expand. Rather than going to a "double session" Sunday School, a second

Sunday School was instituted during the invitation and baptism.

Each Sunday morning, from twelve noon to one o'clock, approximately one hour is spent inviting the unsaved to come forward. Immediately after the invitation, those who have responded are baptized. During the invitation and baptisms the second Sunday School is held.

When the invitation begins at approximately twelve noon, the Sunday School teachers get up and walk out to their classes — most of them teaching the same lesson a second time. Some of the regular Sunday School buses have been gathering pupils to attend this second Sunday School. Also, some of the buses come from such a long distance, they do not arrive in time for the first Sunday School. The same Sunday School rooms and facilities are used twice. At present, the second Sunday School is averaging approximately eight hundred in attendance.

The Making of the Man

Dr. Hyles was asked how he became a great man of God. "I don't consider myself a great man of God. I know I'm a man of God because I'm called of God." He went on to elaborate, because God has given a harvest of souls and blessed his simple preaching. "No man could do it," says Hyles.

He tells the following story that accounts for his approach to preaching. "My father was an alcoholic. He died a drunkard's death in 1950. My mother was a sweet Christian lady and I'm a product of the Sunday School. I never tasted beer, never smoked a cigarette, never said a curse word. I wanted my Dad saved and as a kid I talked to him about being saved. One night, my Dad said he would go to church. I called the pastor and said, 'Would you preach on the second coming; my Dad's coming to church?' (That was always what had scared me and I thought it would move my Dad.) When we got to church, they had choir *contata*. I cried all the way through. Daddy wouldn't come back. That was the only church service my Daddy ever attended."

Hyles went on to conclude, "I said if I ever pastored a church, I would preach Sunday morning and Sunday night. Folks expect the preaching of the Word."

Hyles was converted walking outdoors. Says he, "We were having outdoor services one Sunday night. I got on my knees, by myself. Folks had prayed for me. Folks wondered why I wasn't converted."

The first thing he did for the Lord was to teach a class in training union. He responded, "I taught a teenage boys class when I was nineteen." His next Christian service was being pastor in east Texas when he was twenty-one years old. Hyles went to East Texas Baptist College and Southwestern Baptist Theological Seminary. He came to be pastor of the First Baptist Church in Hammond, Indiana, in 1959.

When Hyles was asked what plans he had for the future, he mentioned, "We're just going to preach the Word of God and win souls. We have no projected five year plan."

Dr. Hyles is Vice President of *The Sword of the Lord* which is used in many pastor's conferences in the United States. He conducts approximately fifteen Sword of the Lord conferences each year, yet seldom has any one else preached in his pulpit. He mentions that he seldom takes a vacation because he loves to preach the Word of God.

When you visit the First Baptist Church of Hammond, Indiana, you are aware of the creative influences of its pastor. The Lord has used him as a human instrument to build the attendance of the Sunday School. The controlling influence for the smooth efficiency resides in Dr. Hyles. First Bapaist Church, Hammond, is the fastest growing Sunday School in the United States. This is because Hyles believes God will work in every service, if given the opportunity. The human reason for growth is the pastor, and the church will continue to grow only as Dr. Hyles continues his energetic outreach.

5

Young and Still Growing

CANTON BAPTIST TEMPLE, CANTON, OHIO

CANTON BAPTIST CHURCH, Canton, Ohio

5

Young and Still Growing

CANTON BAPTIST TEMPLE, CANTON, OHIO

In 1947, twenty-one year old Harold Henniger, was called as pastor of the Canton Baptist Temple in the factory area of Canton, Ohio, under the smoke stacks of Timken Roller Bearing Company. Approximately 150 rallied around this young man whose purpose was to build a great Sunday School. Henniger's preparation included graduation from the Baptist Bible Seminary in Fort Worth, Texas, but more important, he had served on the staff of First Baptist Church, Fort Worth, with Dr. J. Frank Norris. Henniger states, "I learned more Sunday School knowledge in our staff meetings with Dr. Norris than I ever learned in a classroom."

Harold Henniger is the human instrument that God used to raise up Canton Baptist Temple. Dr. John Rawlings of Landmark Baptist Temple stated, "Harold Henniger has one of the greatest young churches in America." He was not stating this because it has over 3,500 in attendance or a two million dollar building. Rawlings went on to give reasons for the greatness of Canton Baptist Temple, — "Because of Harold's spiritual depth, because of his missionary passion, because of his academic training and because of his expository preaching." This church reflects the old proverb, "like priest — like people." Most people believe that ministers in the Bible Baptist Fellowship rant and rave like a holy roller evangelist. Dr. Henniger reads his sermons and visitors are impressed with his incisive preaching and academic depth. Yet the multitudes who stream down the aisle at his invitation reflect his evangelistic zeal.

When Henniger was asked for the key to success in a local church he gave the following points to be followed by a young pastor just starting out in the ministry.

1. Bible exposition.
2. Personal visitation by the pastor.

3. Friendliness — mixing with the people.
4. Business administration.

The following principles were observed in Canton Baptist Temple as factors for its success.

1. *Evangelistic Visitation.* There is great emphasis placed on visitation at Canton Baptist Temple. Soul winning is taught in the Sunday School from cradle roll to the adults. Tuesday is visitation night and over three hundred adults go calling and make almost six hundred visits. In addition to these people, Sunday School teachers make calls on absentees and prospects at their convenience. Henniger states, "There is no substitute for personal visitation."

The visitation program is under the direction of Reverend Ray Rogers, and the success of the visitation program is attributed to him. Each call that is made by a worker or teacher is a total church call. The entire family is contacted and a personal invitation is given for the entire family to attend Sunday School. Reverend Mel Sabaka, the minister of youth, has an active youth evangelistic program. When he first joined the staff six and one-half years ago, he felt the church had to make eight calls to get one person to attend. Today he feels it takes twelve to fourteen calls to get a person to attend.

Sabaka will take one hundred college students out into the parks or onto the beaches on Sunday afternoon to go soul winning. They use Campus Crusade questionnaires to interview people and then present the gospel. Even though Sabaka uses beach and park evangelism, he is skeptical of beach evangelism or coffee house ministry that is not tied to the local church. "Where are the results of such efforts?" asks Sabaka. He goes on to state, "If evangelism is not tied to the local church, it is not Biblical."

Dr. Henniger is a soul winner in every area of life. Recently the author spent several days in Canton and visited restaurants, stores and other businesses. Every contact Henniger made with a cashier or clerk, he took as an opportunity to pass out literature, invite that person to the church and to tell about the Saviour, Jesus Christ. The personal warmth of Henniger is apparent to all who visit the church.

Before and after every church service, Henniger walks through the wide hallways of the church, shaking hands and greeting his people. He stops one lady to ask about her recent illness and a second family to ask about their son in Viet Nam. Henniger knows his church members by name. In personal conversation he refers to his congregation as "my people," reflecting warmth that has developed over twenty-two years of working together for the glory of God.

2. *De-emphasis of Contests and Promotion.* Contrary to most of the other churches in the Baptist Bible Fellowship, Canton Baptist Temple puts little if any emphasis on contests and promotion. Two special attendance drives are held, in the Fall and Spring, but other than this, there are no drives, no gimmicks or promotion. Canton Baptist Temple is built on solid Biblical evangelism and teaching.

Many years ago the congregation was made up of Southerners from the Carolinas and Georgia who came to work in the steel mills of Canton. Those days are past. When driving onto the church parking lot, the modern two story brick building reflects the middle class neighborhood in which the church is now located. Many Northerners have come in and been converted. Henniger states, "The combination of the stability of the Northerner and the warmth of the Southerner makes for a great church."

3. *Musical Program.* Henniger believes one of the necessities in building a large Sunday School is a good musical program. He suggests, "You can't build a church without music, but you can't build a church on music. Music is not a substitute for preaching the Word of God."

Years ago the church music featured gospel quartets from across the Mason-Dixon Line. One of the most successful revival meetings the church ever had was when the Blackwood Brothers sang and Dr. Henniger preached. But today, the music reflects the great hymns but still has warmth and feeling. Reverend Bob Johnson, Minister of Music, is a graduate of Bob Jones University and considered by many to be the best church music director in the Baptist Bible Fellowship. Johnson comments, "We like John Peterson type music." To which Henniger adds, "We don't use the Stamps Baxter music any more."

The live televising of the 10:00 a.m. pastor's class has demanded that the music be up graded. Every Monday morning Johnson views a video tape of the previous broadcast to make improvements for the following week.

4. *Large Sunday School Classes.* Canton Baptist Temple makes maximum use of large Sunday School classes. This method is called

"the master teacher" plan and utilizes the best teachers in the church. Dr. Henniger teaches a Sunday School class in the sanctuary of approximately 1,600 each Sunday morning. This class televised live through the greater Canton area, has a large viewing audience because of the careful Bible teaching and solid sacred music by the hundred voice choir. Recently, a bride and groom class has been formed to bridge the gap between the youth and adult class. Reverend Herbert Koonce is teacher of that class.

Reverend Mel Sabaka teaches over 250 college and career pupils in the youth chapel. There is one class for each age in the junior and senior high school department. These classes average about one hundred pupils in attendance. Sabaka states, "I don't believe in the southern Baptist philosophy of dividing and multiplying." The Baptists in the South have built large Sunday Schools by dividing one large class into at least two smaller classes and using two or more teachers instead of one. They believe this gives a potential of growth. Sabaka answered, "Why tie the hands of my best teachers?" He feels the gifted teacher ought to be able to expand to the maximum of his ability.

5. *Total Church Program.* One of the strengths of Canton Baptist Temple is the well-rounded church program. Some of the churches in the Baptist Bible Fellowship do not have VBS, youth program or an emphasis on camp. Henniger believes in a well-rounded church program in which evangelism comes first, but education is a close second. Last summer the Canton Baptist Temple averaged 1,484 in their VBS program and over 500 in summer camp, cooperating with Ohio Baptist Acres, youth camp. Also, Canton Baptist Temple operates a 6:30 o'clock Sunday evening training program for high schoolers and children. The children's program runs from 7:15 to 8:45 p.m., with primary and beginner children kept in their classes for the evening service.

Canton Baptist Temple has three basketball leagues with eight teams in each league. During the summer there are twelve softball teams. Years ago the church had ball teams in leagues with other churches and the local YMCA. But trouble erupted and the church could not control the actions of other teams, and so formed its own league. The church requires attendance at Sunday School for participation in the weekly recreational activities. Sabaka feels the ball team is a "Bible class" where the captain is responsible for the nurture of each team member. Everything in the church is for the glory of God. He states, "We do not use recreation primarily as an evangelistic outreach but for Christian fellowship and growth of those who are already saved."

6. *Pastoral Leadership.* One of the keys to success in Canton Baptist Temple is strong pastoral leadership. Most of the laymen who were in places of leadership when Harold Henniger came have retired or moved on. As a result they do not remember the young man they called as pastor, but the deacons look up to him as their leader. As a result Henniger stated, "Deacons will do for me what they won't do for the next pastor." He recognizes the place of his leadership and is trying to build the church on solid organization. Canton Baptist Temple has no chairman of the Board of Deasons; Henniger fills this position. Also, Henniger is the chairman of all committees in the church. However, in the coming year, the church will go through a large building program and the pastor does not plan to take the leadership of the building committee but to have a layman elected to the position.

Some of the churches in this study are built on the personality of the pastor. This is not true of Canton Baptist Temple. It is built on the leadership of the pastor. There is a difference between *personality* and *leadership.* Henniger stated, "I lead the church, but at the same time place a lot of confidence in the staff members and delegate responsibilities to them."

7. *Sunday School Buses.* Canton Baptist Temple rents thirteen buses and transports approximately five hundred pupils to Sunday School each week. Children who ride the buses are not from the slums or ghettos. Over half of the riders are youth and adults or retired folks from the city areas.

The average attendance at Canton Baptist Temple is over 3,500 pupils. If Canton Baptist Temple added a fleet of Sunday School buses as other large Sunday Schools, it could easily average over 5,000 in attendance and claim to have one of the largest Sunday Schools in the world. But numbers for the sake of numbers is not the desire of Henniger or the church. The church would rather have a steady growth built on a solid foundation, than an overnight rise in attendance that could fade away just as fast.

Henniger realizes that his leadership would be ineffective without the confidence of his people. To this he states, "Nothing breeds confidence like information." Henniger indicated, "An audit is made of the books each year and the financial books are open to the public." But Henniger qualified this statement, "We don't list every bill in the church bulletin. The average member can't comprehend $600 a month for a light bill. Why, they only pay $8.00 at home." However, the finance committee approves of all these expenditures.

Henniger realizes that the Sunday School could grow faster if they took on a larger debt, but he is unwilling to do so. He feels that his people are not ready for a large indebtedness and would rather have a slow steady growth. He states, "If we fluctuate too much in attendance we create an unstable Sunday School."

8. *The Christian Hall of Fame.* Canton is famous for its Professional Football Hall of Fame. One day the idea struck Henniger, "Why can't we have a Christian Hall of Fame here in Canton?" From this idea grew the Christian Hall of Fame which annually attracts many visitors from various states. Local newspapers and national Christian magazines have given news coverage to this unique presentation of the gospel. Beginning with forty-three original paintings in 1966, the Christian Hall of Fame has grown to a total of seventy-five portraits of outstanding Christian leaders. Only outstanding preachers and evangelists who were true to the inspiration of the Scriptures are placed in the hall. Also, a man must be deceased to be so remembered. Nominations are received from a number of sources and each year approximately six portraits are commissioned to artists by the Board of Directors of the Hall of Fame. Dedication ceremonies are held for each new unveiling.

The massive hallways of the church where the gold framed portraits are hung, give the appearance of a spacious art museum rather than a Sunday School or church. The Christian Hall of Fame is a means of attracting visitors to the church and enrolling Christians into the work of the church.

9. *Youth Ministry.* Visitors to Canton Baptist Temple are impressed with the youthfulness of the staff, as well as of the congregation. The large number of young couples who teach and work in the local church are an encouraging sign for future growth. Many of these couples are attracted because of the outstanding youth ministry of Canton Baptist Temple. Reverend Mel Sabaka superintends the high school and college and career class. Reverend Stan Knisley recently joined the staff as full time Sunday School

superintendent. Before this he was a high school chemistry teacher and was superintendent of the junior high division.

On Thursday evening Sabaka instructs a Bible class of about fifty young single adults. But they are not begged to come. To attend the Bible study, a young person must first attend Sunday School, church, prayer meeting, and go visiting with the group on Saturday afternoon. Sabaka stated, "If a student means business with God, he can come to our Bible study." The dedication causes over 250 to show up for Sunday School class on Sunday morning.

Three years ago the church bought out a supermarket across the much traveled Whipple Avenue and converted it into a youth activities building. The building, beautifully furnished and carpeted throughout with over 10,000 square feet of floor space, reflects the interest the church has in its young people. The next building expansion for the church will include a youth chapel that will seat over five hundred people. Also, the church plans an aluminum arch sidewalk to cross Whipple Avenue and tie the property together.

Sabaka has a going youth program of evangelism, Bible study and fellowship. He stated, "Our activities are not preaching sessions, but are designed to get the youth interested in the church and the Sunday School." He continued, "I may pray on the bus or at the skating rink; I might even bring a short challenge; but our evangelism is done in our Sunday evening youth program or Sunday School class." At a recent Sunday evening youth program five young people made a profession of faith, having been dealt with in the park on Sunday afternoon by young people from the church busy in soul winning.

Canton Baptist Temple was organized in 1938 by Dr. Dallas F. Billington, pastor of Akron Baptist Temple. Akron Baptist Temple has the largest Sunday School in the world, and now this sister church is the second largest in Ohio. The Sunday School program is similar to the one in Akron. This is understandable since Harold Henniger grew up in the Akron church. Dr. Dallas Billington, pastor of Akron Baptist Temple has done his work well, and if given time the Canton church under the leadership of Henniger may climb to be the largest Sunday School in America.

6

A Dream of Ten Thousand in Sunday School

LANDMARK BAPTIST TEMPLE, CINCINNATI, OHIO

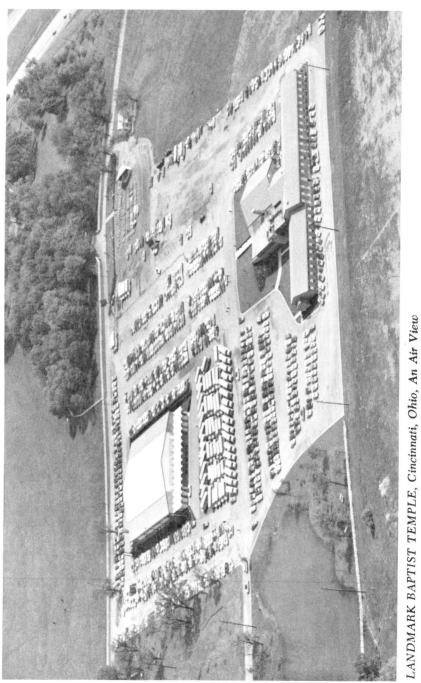

LANDMARK BAPTIST TEMPLE, Cincinnati, Ohio, An Air View

6

A Dream of Ten Thousand in
Sunday School

LANDMARK BAPTIST TEMPLE, CINCINNATI, OHIO

The Landmark Baptist Temple is located on 160 acres of rolling hills, fourteen miles north of downtown Cincinnati, Ohio. Driving onto the grounds you see the fishing lake, baseball diamond, picnic tables, landscaped gardens and inviting woods. The church grounds look more like a park or a college campus. The church has not built a sanctuary yet, but holds services in a 2,278 seat field house; and the youth building, longer than a football field, looks more like a college dormitory than a Sunday School. Also on the grounds is the Liza House, to which Liza escaped in the historic novel, *Uncle Tom's Cabin*.

Dr. John Rawlings became minister in 1951 when the Sunday School was averaging nine hundred. Today, the Sunday School averages somewhat under four thousand in attendance and Rawlings feels that Landmark Baptist Temple has the potential to become the largest Sunday School in the world. He states, "I dreamed for the day with enough land to do what I wanted." There are fifteen acres under blacktop for parking.

For the past several years Dr. Rawlings and a musical quartet of full time staff members travelled throughout forty states holding evangelistic meetings. Their main purpose was winning souls. Also, *The Landmark Hour*, the broadcast of the Sunday evening evangelistic hour, was promoted through their travels. The quartet and other musical groups of the church have produced fourteen record albums and at present are aired over sixty stations. Dr. Rawlings has a vision of putting *The Landmark Hour* on nation wide radio in fifty states, "It will be the first local church broadcast to be heard from coast to coast." The Sunday evening hour is the main evangelistic service of the church. A half-hour is given to music and half-hour to preaching. The attendance at the church averages over two thousand and Dr. Rawlings does most of the preaching.

Last year, the average Sunday School attendance increased by seven hundred over the previous year. This is because Dr. Rawlings decided to stay home and work on his Sunday School rather than travel around the country in evangelistic work.

Potential for Growth

Dr. Rawlings feels that Landmark Baptist Temple has the greatest potential for growth of any Sunday School in America. He states, "There are three requisites for a Sunday School to grow: (1) adequate parking, (2) Sunday School facilities, (3) auditorium." He believes "Anyone can build a Sunday School with hard work, but he must design for unlimited growth." He believes that there are natural ceilings that a church reaches and will have trouble overcoming. Some of these are caused by inadequate organization, small staff or small facilities. Therefore he says, "It's important to take a Sunday School apart and put it back together periodically."

1. *Adequate parking.* Rawlings believes the first criteria to build a large church is to go out and buy adequate acreage. "Absolutely!!!" was his response when asked if he were serious. He went on to say, "Look at the grocery stores in the shopping districts in our suburban neighborhoods. Every one of them has enough parking."

In the late 50's, Rawlings felt his church was dying. He had two preaching services; the Sunday School met in every crack and cranny of the church. There was not enough room for parking. He stated, "We couldn't grow in that neighborhood without space." So Rawlings arranged to purchase 160 acres only two and one-half miles from the original church location. He paid $360,000 in 1958 and conservative estimates indicate he could sell the property for $6,000,000 today. The church finally moved to its new facilities on December 22, 1963, and has been growing ever since.

2. *Sunday School facilities.* Rawlings believes that a church cannot grow without adequate facilities. He states, "If you're growing, you ought not to have a building over 50 per cent filled when it is completed." Recently a youth building with over 65,000 square feet was completed. Also one hundred lay teachers were

added to the staff. These help explain the phenomenal growth in the past year.

Rawlings believes that church growth can be much more rapid today than twenty years ago. He stated, "We can grow to a size in five years that used to take twenty-five years, because of radio, TV, mail, and expressways." It is common for his people to travel the expressway, coming thirty miles to church. But Rawlings feels not just any building will guarantee success. "A lot of success depends upon knowing how to build, so that a church can get maximum use out of its building."

3. *Auditorium.* The present field house will seat 2,260 but he plans to build a sanctuary in the future that will seat 5,000. The Sanctuary will not be the only place where morning worship is held. At present, there are several simultaneous preaching services on the church grounds. There are two thousand adults who meet for the 11:00 A.M. preaching hour in the field house, five hundred teenagers meet in the youth chapel and as many as seven hundred Junior High school pupils gather in their church service. Rawlings is quick to point out, "These are not children's church services like the publishing houses recommend." He goes on to state, "These are preaching services in which staff members lead the service, choirs sing, special music is ministered, offerings are taken and an invitation is given."

Rawlings believes that no Sunday School will reach ten thousand in attendance if it is built on one personality. He believes his formula of several simultaneous preaching services is the formula for reaching an attendance of ten thousand in Sunday School, although his present goal is 5,500 by 1972. Sunday School superintendent, Don Norman stated, "At every staff meeting, we talk in terms of five thousand in Sunday School." Rawlings, who is age fifty-five figures he has fifteen more years to complete his dream at Landmark Baptist Temple. He states, "If our church doesn't grow, it is our own fault. We have every ingredient to build the largest Sunday School in the world."

The Largest Sunday School Bus Fleet in the World

No other church has a larger Sunday School busing ministry than Landmark Baptist Temple. Seventy buses spread out over greater Cincinnati each Sunday morning, one bus going as far as thirty-eight miles away (one way). Contrary to other churches with a heavy busing ministry, Landmark Baptist Temple does not send many of their buses into the slum or ghetto area. They have been successful in middle class and upper class neighborhoods. Rawlings feels that the stability of building on middle class suburbanites is another reason for the great potential of his church.

The church employs a full time mechanic and the repair garage for work on the buses is as up-to-date as any known by Greyhound. Rawlings plans to continue to expand his Sunday School busing ministry. Recently, one bus route was divided into four routes. Four men were sent to work the area and bring in new prospects.

The laws for Sunday School buses in Ohio are just as strict as for public school buses; the state inspector must pass on every bus. This makes Sunday School busing more expensive in Ohio than other states, but Rawlings believes in being as economical as possible. Fuel is bought in bulk and most of the buses are insured for "Sunday only." "Otherwise it would cost us a fortune," states Rawlings. "We drive one-third of a million miles a year with our buses."

Too Many Suckers Spoil the Corn

Dr. John Rawlings understands the dangers of over organizing a local church. He stated "The Southern Baptists are a great Sunday School movement, but they got so involved in organization and Christian education they neglected evangelism." He feels churches should be *reaching*, whereas too many put emphasis on *teaching*. Dr. Rawlings states, "The formula in the great commission is for reaching people and then teaching. Some say I'm anti-intellectural. Not so; I just want to reach people before I teach people. There are too many preachers who are trying to teach and they never reach." Rawlings feels that a church ought to stick to its main job of evangelism. "I'm an old farmer who knows how to grow corn. If you get too many suckers, you stop your corn production. Too many churches add more organization and not more members." Dr. Rawlings states, "A church that is centered in Christian education is not a growing church; it's not a soul winning church. But if you find a church that is interested in evangelism, you find it is interested in teaching the Bible."

Rawlings feels that you can't change the *message* of God, neither can you change the *method* of God. The method is still going out two by two, to present the gospel of Christ to the lost.

When it comes to organization, Rawlings feels there is no substitute for work. He says of himself, "I'm not talented, nor do I have organizational ability. All I have is a desire to work hard."

A Pastor-centered Church

Like many other churches in the Baptist Bible Fellowship, to which the church belongs, Rawlings believes that the pastor is the under shepherd and as such, should give strong leadership to the church. "We have wonderful rapport with the deacons and in my nineteen years here we have had no difficulty." The church has seven deacons and seven trustees. The deacons do not set policy but according to Rawlings, "help to carry out the directives set by the local church." Like all Baptist churches, Rawlings feels that the seat of authority is in the congregation. When the congregation at Landmark Baptist Church had approved the building project, Rawlings signed a contract for $237,000 that did not have to be verified by the congregation. They had given him the power of attorney. Rawlings controls the purse strings of the church, but his reputation is beyond reproach; there is an audit on the books each year. At present, the church owes $1,740,000. Of this, $1,200,000 is held in bonds by his members, showing their confidence in Dr. Rawlings and what they believe is potential for growth in the future. It is in the church's plans to sell approximately one million dollars worth of property they do not need. This will be applied on the present debt.

In all of Dr. Rawlings evangelistic campaigns, he has not accepted a nickel for himself, but receives a modest salary from the church. He returns all love offerings received in evangelistic work to Landmark Baptist Temple. There is an old farm house on the church grounds and Dr. and Mrs. Rawlings occupy the second floor.

There is an obvious love by the staff for their pastor. "The staff enjoys working for pastor," states Don Norman. "The pastor would never ask us to do anything he wouldn't do himself." But Rawlings does demand work. Recently a young man stated, "I wouldn't work for Rawlings for a thousand dollars a week." When Rawlings was told, he replied, "I wouldn't have that young man work for me if he gave me a thousand dollars a week. He's lazy!"

When you visit the Landmark Baptist Church, you are very aware of the driving force of Dr. Rawlings. He stated, "I'm not a dictator, but I've got to set the atmosphere of evangelism." Dr. Rawlings feels that his staff must be a team much like the former Green Bay Packers. He feels he must make the same demands as Vince Lombardi, coach of the Packers, made upon the players. He feels that for his church to be successful, there must be total commitment, total preparation and total team work.

Twenty-one Difficult Sundays a Year

Dr. Rawlings has visited most of the other ten largest Sunday Schools in America, researching their methods. He looks at his church and feels that there are approximately twenty-one difficult Sundays a year that will pull down Sunday School attendance because of snow, ice, rain, Labor Day, Memorial Day, Fourth of July or Christmas. Therefore, he feels he must plan some special days to compensate the loss of attendance. He stated, "If people get in the habit of staying away from church, they will become a permanent drop outs." Therefore, he plans special days to bring his "fringe" members back to church.

One of the biggest outreaches during the year is the Fourth of July picnic where the 160 acre park grounds are utilized. The church brings in helicopters, soft drink wagons, multiple recreation facilities of baseball, fishing, volleyball and games for children. Seven to eight thousand people are reached. Also, the church plans a *Greater Cincinnati Sing Out* in which quartets of Nashville and other portions of the southland participate in a gospel sing. Last August over six thousand attended the *Sing Out* at the outside amphitheater on the church grounds.

The church does not conduct a VBS, or a youth club ministry. Its evangelistic ministry centers around the Sunday School. On Thursday evenings, approximately 250 people show up for visitation and make approximately seven hundred calls on absentees and prospects.

When it comes to promotion, Dr. Rawlings' motto is "Plan it big — keep it simple."

The Landmark Baptist Church has only one adult class that averages 1,200 and meets in the field house. Some might criticize that this is only a preaching service. Reverend Harold Rawlings, son of Dr. John Rawlings, teaches the class; there are four full time staff members who spiritually minister in the class. The class is divided into four sections and records are alphabetized by zip code.

Each of the four sections have four color cards to designate the type of person involved: (1) White card — member. (2) Yellow card — attender. (3) Orange card — worker. (4) Blue card — prospect. The four workers in the adult section spend their time phoning, visiting, and following up contacts within the large class.

There is one class for each year in the Junior high and Senior high school class. These classes average in size from one hundred to two hundred pupils. Some might criticize the size of these large classes, desiring to divide them into smaller units. Full time staff members of the church teach each of these classes. In addition, there are approximately thirty-six adult lay workers in each class to help with counseling, discipline, meeting new students and the clerical work. Dr. Rawlings feels thirty-six adult counselors per class will give better results, better discipline and better personal contact with the high school pupils. The interaction of the adult lay workers and the staff members form a modified team teaching situation.

About five years ago, a study of the records indicated Landmark Baptist Church was losing its teenagers. As a result, a new emphasis was made in youth work. Every Saturday night there is a youth service at the church. Also, the youth were moved into the chapels for their own church service (approximately 1,400). The youth have their own choir, special music and ushers. However, the staff member takes charge of the service and adult counselors deal with those who come forward for salvation. High schoolers hear an adult sermon every Sunday morning, not "watered down to youth." Dr. Rawlings feels the gospel is relevant and the Word of God should be preached to high school young people.

The Seventies Could Be the Greatest in Church Age

According to Dr. Rawlings, "The next ten years could be the greatest age in the life of the church." He feels that the Independent Baptist Churches who are rapidly growing, are doing so through Sunday School evangelism. The Book of Acts mentions large crowds of three thousand and five thousand. Rawlings feels that in the next ten years in the Baptist Bible Fellowship alone, there will be over twenty-five churches averaging three thousand in Sunday School. In spite of sin, the world, and the Devil, Dr. Rawlings feels the next ten years will be the greatest of all ages in which to minister for God.

7

Sunday School with a Past and a Potential

TEMPLE BAPTIST CHURCH, DETROIT, MICHIGAN

TEMPLE BAPTIST CHURCH, Detroit, Michigan

7

Sunday School with a Past and a Potential

Temple Baptist Church grew out of a mission Sunday School established in 1892. Since that time, there have been seven pastors, the most recent being: Dr. Albert Johnson, 1925-1934; Dr. J. Frank Norris, 1935-1950; and Dr. G. Beauchamp Vick, present pastor. However, the church's greatest growth and outreach was accomplished under the leadership of Dr. Vick, who became General Superintendent and song leader in 1936, co-pastor in 1947, and pastor in 1950.

Three Periods of History

Temple Baptist Church has had three periods in its great history. The first period was one of growth — from 1937 to the mid 1950's when Temple Baptist Church became one of the largest churches in America. In 1955, the Christmas issue of *Life* magazine ran a two page photograph of the congregation, stating it was one of the largest Sunday Schools in the world. The Sunday School was averaging about five thousand in attendance. The second period saw a decline. The neighborhood changed with the inhabitants moving out. A process of deterioration set in and institutional blight spread over the neighborhood. The building was subject to vandalism and people who attended services at night were attacked physically. As a result there was a hesitancy on the part of new people to come into the neighborhood. Those who were in the church continued, but without new faces to replace those who moved the attendance dipped to approximately 3,000.

The third period of growth in the church began in the fall of 1968. A new four million dollar building was completed in the suburbs.

On October 27, 1968, a crowd of over seven thousand witnessed the dedication. The dedication of the new building with its four acres of Sunday School rooms, made news. Three television stations sent crews to the dedication. Former members of the congregation from all over America attended the service. Extra chairs were set up all over the auditorium and many had to see the service in the chapel via closed circuit television. Cars were lined bumper to bumper in each direction. The public recognition for this great church was due to its faithfulness in evangelism over the years.

The Leadership of Dr. G. Beauchamp Vick

This fantastic growth came through the ministry of Dr. G. Beauchamp Vick, born in Russellville, Kentucky, in 1901. The son of a lawyer and later pastor, Dr. Vick wanted to attend West Point and have a career in the military, but God had other plans.

The Sunday School at Temple Baptist Church averaged approximately seven hundred when Dr. Vick came to Temple Baptist Church. His first task was to diagnose the Sunday School. He set up a thirty minute appointment with every Sunday School teacher and worker. The task was so time consuming, he brought a quart of milk and a sandwich to the office and began his day at 9:00 in the morning and interviewed his workers until 10:00 at night.

Dr. Vick faced the summer slump when attendance usually dipped to three hundred in attendance and many teachers went on their vacations. Dr. Vick stated that one of his first duties was, "to motivate each worker to serve his responsibility before God." Because he emphasized evangelism and responsibility, the attendance climbed to over eleven hundred in August rather than taking its usual nose dive.

Dr. Vick indicates the human side of growth for the early church and for today is found in Acts 5:42, "and daily in the temple and in every house, they ceased not to teach and preach Jesus Christ." Dr. Vick reasoned that Jesus began with twelve and His work grew to three thousand persons on the day of Pentecost and to five thousand persons later on; why couldn't Temple Baptist Church?

He feels that numbers are important because they are put in the Bible. "A church should be concerned about numbers." He adds, "I am concerned about a *number* of people for Christ." Dr. Vick points to the emphasis on numbers in the book of Acts, as support for the emphasis Temple Baptist Church makes on growth. The following number progression in Acts give him guidelines for growth.

Acts 1:15 — 120 disciples

Acts 2:41 — 3,120 (120 disciples plus 3,000 conversions)

Acts 2:47 — "added to the church daily"

Acts 4:4 — about 5,000

Acts 5:14 — multitudes

Acts 6:1 — "the number of the disciples was multiplied."

Acts 6:7 — "the number of the disciples multiplied greatly."

Dr. Vick looks upon the book of Acts as the handbook for the Sunday School growth. Acts 9 and 10 include the records of two visits: one made by a layman in the home of Judas on a street called Straight in Damascus, and the other made by a preacher, Simon Peter, in the home of Cornelius, the centurian in Caesarea.

Visitation — Key to Growth

Visitation is the key to success at Temple Baptist Church. Joe Wade, Sunday School superintendent, states, "The whole program of Sunday School is geared to visitation and soul winning." From 90 per cent to 96 per cent of those who came forward professing faith in Christ did so through Sunday School visitation. Most of these have already been saved in the home through the instrumentality of someone who had gone visiting.

On Monday evening, approximately 300 to 450 people will be present for visitation supper. The meal prepared by the church kitchen staff costs a nominal 50¢ per person. After the meal the workers first go to their individual Sunday School classrooms. Here they are instructed on *how* and *whom* to visit. The adults go out as couples, visiting couples. Where a husband and wife are not present, two men will go together. They leave around seven p.m. and make as many calls as possible. The purpose of the calls is soul winning, not merely to invite people to church.

The church does not run a weekly club program nor does it have a summer vacation Bible school program. Dr. Vick feels that Christian education does not build a large church but soul winning does. The total program centers around visitation and Sunday School.

Sunday School Organization

Temple Baptist Church does not use Sunday School literature from a Sunday School publishing house. Dr. Vick and Joe Wade decide upon the curriculum for the Sunday School. The lesson schedules are printed a small size so they will fit into a Bible. First on Wednesday evening, either Joe Wade of Dr. Vick teach the Sunday School lesson to the teachers. Afterwards, from 7:00 to 7:30 p.m. departmental meetings are held where they discuss problems pertinent to the age group. Also the lesson is applied to the particular age. All teachers join the congregation for the prayer meeting at 7:30 p.m.

Emphasis is put on adults, so that 52 per cent of the Sunday School population are adult age. Temple Baptist Church has seven adult married classes. These range in attendance from one hundred to five hundred. Dr. Vick feels that this is wiser than to include all adults in one large class which he believes almost invariably degenerates into a second-rate preaching service.

Temple Baptist Church does not give the invitation in the Sunday School class. Dr. Vick feels, "Sunday School is the seed sowing service; the preaching service is the harvest." But no church service is concluded without an invitation.

At one time Temple Baptist Church had a large busing program, but over the years it has been phased out. Today there are only five buses that bring in approximately three hundred people. Most of these result from the relocation of the church the past year, and people are bused from the old neighborhood.

When Dr. Vick was asked whether a young church should go into busing he replied, "Don't do without busing, but don't depend upon it completely." His major complaint against busing was that this brought in too large a proportion of children. He stated, "I'm sick of little kiddie emphasis in Sunday School. Winning kids is necessary, but when you win the father and mother to Christ, you get the whole family." When this observer visited the church, eight came forward in the evening service. Only one was a child.

Strong Pastoral Leadership

Dr. Vick believes the pastor should not be a dictator, but should be a strong leader. He went on to say, "A Baptist church is a democracy. The pastor is the big democrat," he added with a smile. Vick feels that too often the pastor is treated as a hireling, and as an errand boy for the deacons. This he believes is wrong. The pastor is God's chosen servant. The deacons are busy all day long about something other than church. They should not meet briefly to tell the pastor how to run the church. Vick went on to say, "If a deacon knows how to run a church he ought to be the pastor." Vick was not being facetious, for he believes that there is a place in full-time service for dedicated laymen. Some of the ordained men on his staff were once laymen who worked in his church.

However, Vick is not insensitive in dealing with lay leadership in his church. He takes the deacons into his confidence. They pray together, discuss and plan together. However, in financial matters, the pastor should be the controller or business manager of the church. Vick said, "I keep in close touch with the finances, but I don't sign any checks, nor do I have the combination to the safe." Three members of the Finance Committee must countersign a check. Vick gets a financial report once a week, and meets with seven deacons who form the Finance Committee to advise him in decisions. He feels the only way to run the finances of a local church are: (1) people must give by the Scriptural method of tithing, (2) the pastor must establish confidence by faithful administration of God's treasure, and (3) regular weekly reports and an annual audit must be made to the membership concerning the disposition of funds.

The process whereby Temple Baptist Church sold its downtown property on Grand River and moved to the suburbs reflect the attitude of Dr. Vick to his leadership "trust" and the financing of the local church.

The downtown church was in an undesirable neighborhood. Some of the ladies had been accosted as they attended church in spite of the fact that the parking lots were illuminated and guards were posted for the security of the people. Vandalism on parked cars was soaring and many people were leaving the church because they were afraid of the neighborhood.

"I realized we would have to move," stated Dr. Vick. He proceeded to put every family name on a 3 x 5 card and divided the names according to postal zones. By drawing a large map he found that the geographical center of the church membership was north of Ford Road, south of six Mile Road, near Telegraph Road.

He personally surveyed the area, feeling that ten acres of ground was the minimum requirement for the new church. There were only three pieces of property available within a designated area.

A farmer wanted $300,000 for 16½ acres, and Dr. Vick secured an option on the property. The seven deacons on the finance committee were brought into his confidence, and told of his plans. Dr. Vick undertook a courageous decision. According to him, "I risked my whole ministry on the move of the church." On Sunday morning, November 21, 1965, he announced to the congregation that a business meeting would be held after the evening service. Also, he made the same announcement in the evening service inasmuch as there needed to be two announcements of a business meeting to make it legal.

Before the evening service, Vick met with his forty deacons and explained to them the proposed move.

During the business meeting, Dr. Vick asked for three votes by the congregation: (1) that they buy the sixteen acres on West Chicago Avenue and Telegraph Road, (2) that he be given the right to negotiate the sale of the downtown property, and (3) that the church begin on a four million dollar project under the direction of a building committee.

The deacons sat in the choir loft as Dr. Vick carefully laid out the alternatives concerning the move. It is not a light matter, to ask a congregation to move, especially involving a four million dollar building.

That evening only two questions came from the floor. (1) What was the growing trend of the population of the city? The answer was that the church would be in the center of the suburban population. (2) Would some of the older folks be able to find transportation to the new church? Of course, the answer was "yes."

Over two thousand folks voted unanimously to approve the pastor's request, reflecting great confidence in their leader. The building was ultimately sold to the school board of Detroit for $1,150,000. The financing of the church was arranged by Dr. Vick and the mortgage will be paid off in five years.

The four million dollar building is a testimony to the desire on the part of the people to honor God with the very best. The sanctuary has 4,500 theater seats. When asked why they did not use pews, Joe Wade, Sunday School superintendent replied, "This is a soul winning church, and we find it easier to do personal work and more convenient for those who wish to respond to the invitation when seats are used." The carpeted aisles and blue velvet seats give an atmosphere of luxury. However, the choir does not wear robes and there is no sign of liturgy. To this, Dr. Vick replied, "If this church gets too fancy, I'll sprinkle sawdust up and down the aisle and remind the folks that this is an evangelistic tabernacle."

In thirty-three years there has not been one Sunday in which some did not respond to the invitation.

The Influence of Temple Baptist Church

The outreach of Temple Baptist Church is greater than its Sunday School. Over 275 young men have entered either the missionary service or full time pastorate from the church. Dr. Vick states, "We don't know how many churches we have established, but almost every Baptist church in Detroit has some who were saved in Temple Baptist Church."

Dr. Vick is president of the Baptist Bible College in Springfield, Missouri, which has an attendance of 1,400 full time students. This task is in addition to being pastor of the Temple Baptist Church. But Vick believes the best ministers are home grown products. Most of the men who work on his staff were laymen who were effective workers in Temple Baptist Church. "The people knew them and they knew the church," stated Joe Wade. Some of the men went away to Bible College or Seminary but they came back and worked in the local church. They are ordained and perform the weddings and funerals of the church.

The church has vitality and vision. In six months, since the dedication of the new building, the attendance has jumped about five hundred, so that now the Temple Baptist Church is averaging somewhat under 4,000 in Sunday School. However, the figure of 3,400 attendance for the reporting period is averaged from a low attendance of 2,900 and a high attendance of 3,900. For the past ten years, Temple Baptist Church has averaged approximately 4,400 in Sunday School. In a short period of time the Sunday School will probably recover the lost attendance and again reach its high standing. Some churches are known by their past, other churches are known by their future. Temple Baptist Church has a Sunday School with a *past* and a *potential.*

8

A Typical American Sunday School with a Total Educational Program

FIRST BAPTIST CHURCH, VAN NUYS, CALIFORNIA

FIRST BAPTIST CHURCH OF VAN NUYS, Van Nuys, California

8

A Typical American Sunday School with a Total Educational Program

FIRST BAPTIST CHURCH, VAN NUYS, CALIFORNIA

The First Baptist Church of Van Nuys, California, comes closer than any of the other churches in this study of being a typical American church. Located in the suburbs of the San Fernando Valley, the church has a well-rounded total church program, ministering to the whole student, at every age level, meeting individual and neighborhood needs. The church ministers in outreach to the deaf, blind, handicapped groups, and senior citizens. The elementary school located on the church property enrolls almost four hundred students, a Christian book store supplies literature and news sheets keep the clientele up-to-date on church news. The church has an outstanding camp and conference grounds in the San Bernardino Mountains at Lake Arrowhead. The church basketball, volleyball and softball leagues minister to the recreational needs of man, highlighted by the all important church-sponsored golf tournaments. Special training classes, annual mission conference, ladies missionary society, graded choirs, arts and crafts classes, church music conferences and evangelistic outreach all qualify First Baptist Church of Van Nuys as a *typical American Sunday School with a total church program.*

When Dr. Harold L. Fickett, Jr. came as pastor in 1959 he took as his motto, "A Church with a Vision." He built steadily, founding church growth upon the Sunday School. Dr. Fickett stated in *Moody Monthly,* April, 1968, "Organizationally speaking, the Sunday School is still the greatest force for outreach in the church today." The church membership has increased by 4,100 since Dr. Fickett came, and recently he baptized his three thousandth person since coming to Van Nuys.

Most of the ministers in the ten largest Sunday Schools have served only one church — the one they presently serve. Dr. Fickett has pastored several churches in Massachusetts, New Jersey, Texas, Pennsylvania and California. He earned a Th.D. degree from Eastern Baptist Theological Seminary, and also served as a United States Naval Chaplain, taking part in the battles of Iwo Jima and Okinawa as an attack transport chaplain during the Second World War. Fickett was discharged with the rank of Lieutenant Commander from the Naval Reserve in 1950.

Fickett loves to preach. Recently he stated in a pastoral letter to his people:

> God called me to preach; I eat, sleep and think preaching; I'd rather do this than anything else, and when you tell me that your lives have been enriched through the message which the Lord has given me, it makes me want to do a better job in the pulpit for the Saviour in 1969 than I have done in 1968.

Organization and Administration. Unlike the other churches in this study, First Baptist Church of Van Nuys has an extensive organizational structure. Dr. Fickett states, "Organization and administration have played an important role in the building of our church attendance. On the human level I would place this right at the top." The program, headed by five full time pastors, reaches into every aspect of pupil's lives. Fickett wrote in the church newspaper, "People often ask why the Sunday School at First Baptist Church is continually growing numerically. We believe one of the answers to be that our Sunday School classes are well organized, planned and productive so that people who come find it to be a happy experience." The church has an abundance of meetings reflecting the extensive organization. The church bulletin for February 16, 1969, lists sixty-four different meetings held at the church during the week, not counting those regularly scheduled, but not announced. Some of the unusual meetings were as follows:

Bowling for the Blind
Youth Orchestra
Oil Painting Class
CCC-Roaring Twenties Bible Study
Jolly 60's
Women's Handbell Choir
Model Airplane Club
Harmonica Choir Rehearsal

Jewish-Christian Bible Discussion
Jr. High Handbell Choir
Horseback Riding
Civil Air Patrol Meeting
Finger Spelling Class
Certain Sounds Band Rehearsal

An examination of the church's organizational plan shows that every agency reports directly to the pastor who in turn reports to the congregation.

The church does not have a Board of Christian Education to supervise its Sunday School. Fickett states, "Our Christian Education staff does that." Also, there is no lay Sunday School superintendent in the church. Instead, they have a paid coordinator at the head of each division in the Sunday School.

Singing to the Glory of God. The weekly newspaper of First Baptist Church of September 18, 1968, joyfully invites the people to "join the choir." You would have a hard time saying no in this church, for there are thirty-three musical groups (vocal and instrumental) and some group is practicing almost every day of the week. If you have a five-year-old kindergartener, he could join one of the three cherub choirs that meets on Tuesday afternoon. If you have children in any other department of the Sunday School up through the college class, there is a choir waiting for them. Also, if you have a grandmother living with you, she could join the "Jolly 60's" choir for senior citizens.

John Gustafson, Minister of Music, directs the thirty-three choirs and instrumental groups involving 1,400 people. He is assisted by six staff members and a dedicated corps of workers. Directors, pianists, choir mothers, choir dads, and assistant directors are needed for each group.

A Full Recreational Program. The church conducts its own Little League for the small boys in baseball, football and basketball. Similar recreational programs are available at the junior high, high school, college, and the men's level. The annual golf tournament seems to be one of the highlights of the recreational year.

The church has a gymnasium and is planning to construct a building with a large roller skating rink, eight bowling lanes, two handball courts, and a number of game rooms. First Baptist Church of Van Nuys attempts to minister to the entire man. Approximately twelve hundred students are involved in the recreational outreach of the church.

Arrowpines is the church camp facility that is used year round. Last summer 1,750 students enrolled in the summer camping program. Almost every weekend during the winter, one of the church groups plans a retreat in Arrowpines. Some of these retreats are recreational, others are church planning, while still others are training in nature. These activities fall under the direction of the Minister of Weekday Activities.

The Training Program. Last fall a five day leadership training institute prepared workers for their age level department for the Sunday School. The courses were taught by outstanding leaders such as Dr. John Sizemore of the Southern Baptist Convention and Rodney Toeves of Gospel Light Publications. Adult training classes are held every Sunday evening before the evening service. The total training union program reaches fifteen hundred from the junior level, right up through adults. The Southern Baptist Training Union material is the basic core; however, materials from several other publishing houses are used.

Enrollment. The church places much emphasis on enrolling new members in the Sunday school. A brochure stated, "Another way of stating enrollment is, *possibilities.*" The church believes that it is possible to have in attendance all those who are enrolled. Therefore, the goal is to enroll more people in Sunday School for Jesus Christ. The pastor indicated, "Our goal should naturally be to keep our attendance reaching toward the enrollment."

Visitation. The church has an all day visitation program on Thursday, utilizing some five hundred trained workers to do prospect calling. Women do calling during the day and men, joined by women who were not available during the day, go out visiting in the evening. Every organized Sunday School class in the adult department has a concentrated visitation program in which close contact is kept with all the members of the group, plus visitation of absentees. This program extends to all of the Sunday School departments. The church estimates that it makes approximately a thousand calls a week by its lay workers. The full time staff member makes approximately one hundred home visits per week.

Goal Setting. The church believes in setting goals for each and every department and agency of its vast outreach. Goal setting applies also to financial income. In the last quarter of 1968 a goal of $20,000 per Sunday was set and the weekly tabulation was made in the church bulletin to reveal how close the offering came to the goal; The church went well over the goal.

Goal setting applies to Sunday School attendance. During the "March to Sunday School in March" contest, Lowell Brown, Minister of Education stated, "The Christian Education Department has established a unique goal of 3,333 average attendance during the month of March. That is an increase of 7½ per cent over last year during March. It is obvious from our goal that the number 3 is the key to our program. Everything is designated in 3's. For example, we have established 3 methods of growth:

Home visitation
Phone Campaign
Mail Contacts

Brown went on to state that by utilizing these methods, we believe we will obtain a 3-fold result:

An increased enrollment
Increased attendance
New prospects.

Brown established an attendance goal for each department in the Sunday School. The goal for each department was set on a 7½ per cent increase and printed in the church bulletin. The actual attendance was printed so that the department could tell whether they had met the goal or not — so could everyone else. For the month the church school averaged 3,467, well over the goal for 3,333.

The Building. Since Dr. Fickett has become pastor of the church, a new educational building of 16,000 square feet has been built. In 1965 a new $1,300,000 sanctuary was dedicated. The organ recital in dedication was one of the high points of occupying the new sanctuary. The pipe organ was built by Sasavante Freres Ltd. of Saint-Hyacinthe, Quebec, Canada. The First Baptist Church emphasizes its worship *sanctuary*, when some of the other churches in this study use the term, *auditorium*. They tend to de-emphasize anything dealing with formalism.

The Certain Sounds, Evangelistic Outreach of College and Career Youth. A group of two hundred college and career young adults have banded together for an exciting adventure in fellowship and evangelism. During spring holidays, Fourth of July and Labor Day weekends, the young adults from the church launch an evangelistic thrust into Palm Springs, Catalina, or one of the other vacation resorts that attracts young people of California. Approximately eighty young people usually take part in one of these campaigns. There are sixteen singers and a twelve piece band, concentrating on folk music with just a sprinkling of songs of spiritual vein. Music provides the attraction, with secular songs such as "Up, Up, and Away" and "Born Free." Testimonies concerning faith in Jesus Christ are given by the young people and a time of intense personal witnessing follows.

The Certain Sounds get booed, heckled and interrogated. But Labor Day weekend, 1967, 225 signed cards indicating acceptance of Jesus Christ as personal saviour.

The group might rent an empty night club, set up a band stand on a beach or any place that is allowable. When the group was in Palm Springs, civic organizations showed their appreciation by presenting the group a check for $100 and an open invitation to return. The Catalina city council arranged round trip tickets on the steamer for the entire group for a return trip.

"A Church with a Vision" realizes that planning is necessary to make a vision become reality. A church brochure states, "While ours is not a crassly commercial enterprise, we must recognize that we are meeting the needs of people through the Person of Christ and through the programs and activities we develop to serve His converts." The church congregation is challenged to win the one million people in the San Fernando Valley to Christ. At the same time, the congregation is challenged. During the next ten years the population in the valley will double, and the church also expects to double. The outreach of the church will go forward, states the brochure if the four following points are followed:

1. Win people to Christ.

2. Teach them to become mature and dedicated Christians, understanding God's will for their lives.

3. Make each witness effective in the community.

4. Provide Christians with a wide variety of opportunities for participation and fellowship.

First Baptist Church has grown because of its total church program reaching all needs of man in every section of the neighborhood. Each Sunday School department and church agency has shown consistent year by year increase, thus proving that the church with a well-rounded, total church program can bring growth in Sunday School attendance.

9

The Youngest Sunday School in the Ten Largest

THOMAS ROAD BAPTIST CHURCH, LYNCHBURG, VIRGINIA

NEW SANCTUARY AND CHAPEL, Thomas Road Baptist Church

ADULT BIBLE CLASS on Thirteenth Anniversary, June 8, 1969

9

The Youngest Sunday School
in the Ten Largest

THOMAS ROAD BAPTIST CHURCH, LYNCHBURG, VIRGINIA

The youngest church among the ten largest is Thomas Road Baptist Church, Lynchburg, Virginia. Dr. Jerry Falwell, pastor and founder, knows the Lynchburg area, having been born and raised in the area. Falwell was a pre-mechanical engineering major at Lynchburg College. The radio ministry of Dr. Charles Fuller, Old Fashioned Revival Hour, was used of God to bring Falwell under the conviction of the Holy Spirit. On January 20, 1952, he visited a local church and for the first time heard the gospel preached just as Dr. Fuller had presented it, and was converted that same night. Immediately the Holy Spirit spoke to Falwell's heart about full time Christian service and he enrolled at the Baptist Bible College, Springfield, Missouri.

During his training at Springfield, Falwell would drive to Kansas City, some two hundred miles, to minister with Dr. Wendell Zimmerman, pastor of the Kansas City Baptist Temple. As God blessed the preaching opportunities, Falwell was assured that God was calling him into a full time pastoral ministry.

He graduated from Bible College in May, 1956, and some Christian friends invited him to Macon, Georgia, to help establish a local church. Falwell wanted to spend several weeks at home in Lynchburg with his family before going on to start the new venture in Georgia. In Lynchburg he was confronted with the opportunity of establishing a church in his own town. Falwell was mindful that "a prophet is not without honor save in his own country" but he felt this was God's will.

The Thomas Road Baptist Church was formed on June 21, 1956, in a rented school building and later in a rented building on the present site. The former grocery store and soft drink bottling company was used as the launching pad to build one of the fastest growing Sunday Schools in the United States. The building was completely rennovated and small educational unit added.

Within a year, a new auditorium seating six hundred and an educational unit were built on the original property. Seven years later, 1964, a new sanctuary had to be built and was dedicated in the spring with almost two thousand in attendance.

At present, Thomas Road Baptist Church is endeavoring to raise $300,000 to build a sanctuary to seat three thousand for the morning service which now flows over into three buildings. Many people sit in extra chairs in every aisle and corner, many of them unable to see the pulpit. A church brochure states, "Many others have stated that they plan to come to our services when *we get more space.*"

The church has grown because of communication and outreach, which is reflected by a sixty-minute television program sponsored by the church; Elim Home for Alcoholics; Treasure Island, a Christian academy, a private day school with approximately two hundred students (kindergarten through grade six); and a book and Bible center ministry through the local church. Attached to this is the Old Time Gospel Hour Press employing two full time printers where thousands of books, and publicity extends the ministry of the church into greater Lynchburg and other areas.

Pastoral Leadership

Falwell was asked why the church has been successful. To this he answered, "God has honored a combination of faithfulness to His Word, continuous dependence upon prayer, and hard work. We have prayed as though everything depended upon God; we have preached, visited, and worked as though everything depended upon us."

Each of the ten largest Sunday Schools has been built upon the leadership and energy of one man. Thomas Road Baptist Church is no exception. Falwell believes that the pastor is God's man to lead His flock. The deacons meet monthly, at which time Falwell counsels and invites each of them to relate what God is saying to them concerning the church and its ministry. The matters are discussed freely and the deacons pray much together. However, Falwell indicates, "The board has always felt inclined to accept my direction in matters relating to church policy." Matters of important business, such as purchasing property or erecting buildings, are taken to the congregation for approval. The congregation has always sanctioned the suggestions of the board and pastor. Falwell believes that, "A pastor should not be a dictator but he should be a spiritual leader."

Rev. James Soward, co-pastor, is also the Sunday School superintendent. Falwell and Soward originate most of the promotional ideas and add the motivational impetus for growth.

Although Falwell gives the church strong leadership, he delegates responsibility to superintendents, teachers and workers, and gives them a sense of participation in the ministry. The Sunday School staff meets together weekly, at which time Falwell tries to inspire them to action. Also, he meets with the full time staff each morning, Monday through Friday at 8:30, for prayer and discussion. He is in his office each morning for the administration of church affairs.

A Church Reaches Out

Contrary to the other churches in this study, Thomas Road Baptist Church does not have a regular organized visitation night. Sunday School teachers are asked to spend at least two hours a week in house to house visitation. Bus captains are required to spend three hours a week. They go at their convenience. The enthusiasm of Falwell compels people to go beyond this basic requirement. In every service, Falwell urges the people to witness daily, on the job, at school, and in their communities. He states, "Participation by hundreds of people in daily witnessing is the key to our continual Sunday School and church growth."

Falwell feels strongly that "Sunday School teachers should indoctrinate Biblical truth, not simply discuss the issues of Biblical truth." At this place, he is more evangelistic-centered than educationally centered. Falwell states, "Sunday School teachers of our seven adult classes spend the entire time in lecturing or presenting the Bible message for that day."

The church has just completed a new educational building with room for two thousand students. The church has massive plans for the future. In fact, two more educational buildings are already under construction at a cost of $460,000. A sanctuary that would seat over three thousand persons is also under construction at a cost of $900,000. The church is building all three buildings simultaneously to permit growth to five thousand in Sunday School. The additional space should be available by Fall, 1970. At present the church is situated on a ten acre tract of land and there are plans to secure additional property for expansion.

The Sunday School buildings are used five days a week by The Lynchburg Christian Academy. Falwell believes that it is poor stewardship to take, "hundreds of thousands of dollars in buildings and use them for only one hour a week in Sunday School." The Academy organized in 1966 hires only teachers that meet certification set by the state of Virginia. The school receives no federal assistance and claims to be supported by no one particular church. However, Thomas Road Baptist Church is a heavy contributor. Many individuals give support. Also, over four hundred students are expected for the Fall semester, 1969. The statement of purpose for the school is "to give Christian training along with solid academic foundation in the basic fundamentals of learning for the average and above average student."

The Elim Home for Alcoholics is now in its tenth year of operation. The statement of approach is simple, "Elim Home treats alcoholism as sin. Jesus Christ is presented as the only hope of deliverence." The home has dormitory rooms for eighteen men, a study, a living room, a kitchen, a dining room and a large workshop. The brochure offers, "Adequate housing for the men where physical, social and spiritual needs may be met in an atmosphere of love, discipline and guidance to be given under proper direction and supervision."

Each day, activities center around Bible study, prayer, and counseling. Men are exhorted to consistency in the Christian life. The purpose of Elim Home is to restore men to the state of physical, mental, and moral health so he may return to an active, useful and well-balanced life and become a productive member of his family, community and society.

The men in Elim Home are active in the maintenance work of Thomas Road Baptist Church. They repair, remodel, paint and do much carpenter work for the church. They also assist in the printshop. Through the years the men have built much of the furniture used in the educational building.

In addition to the woodworking shop, each man is assigned maintenance, laundry and other housekeeping responsibilities. It is felt that responsibility brings about maturity.

Also, Hope Aglow Halfway House for prison releasees is in its second year of operation. Like the aims of Elim Home, Hope

Aglow Halfway House had the purpose of returning a man to physical, moral and spiritual health.

Rev. Ed. Martin, one of the associate pastors, directs the work within the prisons and jails. Bible correspondence courses are planned to involve a man in study of the Word of God. The rehabilitation efforts with the releasees has been a unique endeavor among fundamental churches.

Treasure Island, the Christian youth camp, only ten minutes away from the church, is located on an island in the middle of the James River near downtown Lynchburg. All of the necessities for good recreational programs are provided: gymnasium, ball field, paved tennis courts, and swimming pool. Like the other endeavors of Thomas Road Baptist Church, the purpose of Treasure Island is to lead youth to a knowledge of Christ, promote Christian living and provide a wholesome time of fun and recreation. The camp is operated in an efficient manner, and receives donations from churches, civic organizations, and parents to help maintain its outreach. Last summer, approximately two thousand campers were enrolled in the ten week camp period.

The televisions outreach results in a sixty-minute program, *The Old Time Gospel Hour,* and is presently viewed on several stations in cities other than Lynchburg. Actually, the eleven o'clock church service is produced on video tape for re-play in other cities. Falwell indicates *The Old Time Gospel Hour* is "replayed at early Sunday morning hours, not competing with Sunday School and church services elsewhere."

The Old Time Gospel Hour is edited so that the programs are interesting to those who are not church members at Thomas Road Baptist Church. The church owns three television cameras and all of the necessary control room equipment, amounting to $200,000 in equipment. The television crew is maintained by a staff of dedicated church laymen, who share the responsibility of producing the program. This is contrary to many local churches that are branching into the television, using technicians from the local TV station.

God has blessed the Thomas Road Baptist Church in its television outreach. Falwell indicates, "You would be thrilled if you could sit at my desk . . . answer my phone . . . and listen as people tell me what the Lord has done for them as a result of their watching the *Old Time Gospel Hour* telecast." Letters of gratitude are received every day from people who have been converted through watching the program in their homes. A brochure from the church indicates, "Alcoholics have ceased to drink, divorce actions have been stopped, and separated families have been brought back together. These are just a few of the many thrilling testimonies of what Christ can do to meet any need in the lives of individuals when given a chance. This is why we put so much emphasis on our television ministry."

Falwell indicates $30,000 a year is needed for each station to air the *Old Time Gospel Hour*. He encourages all those who watch the program through TV to send in gifts for its support.

At the writing of this book, Thomas Road Baptist Church is actually running seventeen bus routes and bringing approximately eight hundred children per Sunday to the church. Some of the churches in the ten largest Sunday Schools are phasing out their bus ministry; however, Falwell plans to expand its outreach. They plan to buy fifteen more buses in the immediate future which according to Falwell, will bring one thousand pupils to Sunday School, each week. Within the following year, so states Falwell, "It is our intention to be busing two thousand pupils each week into our Sunday School." As one views the tremendous expansion already evidenced at Thomas Road Baptist Church, there is little doubt that the two thousand people by bus will not be realized.

The 1970's is still the age of miracles, and we witness again and again the work of the power of God. Thomas Road Baptist Church has demonstrated the effectiveness of old fashioned techniques in a modern age. If its growth is as spectacular in the next decade as in the past decade, this will be the largest Sunday School in America. If all churches were as spectacular in growth as Thomas Road Baptist Church, America would have a sweeping revival.

10

The Whole Man through the Total Educational Program

CALVARY TEMPLE, DENVER, COLORADO

CALVARY TEMPLE, Denver, Colorado

10

The Whole Man through the Total Educational Program

CALVARY TEMPLE, DENVER, COLORADO

Dr. Charles Blair was called to a small struggling church in Denver, Colorado. It consisted of thirty-two adult members, and had an annual income of $1,400, not sufficient to pay a full time salary to the minister. That was 1947. Now, twenty-two years later, Calvary Temple has a church membership of approximately four thousand, a weekly attendance of almost twenty-five hundred, with gifts last year totalling $869,475. God took charge of money and attendance problems in those early years. He continues to do so in the present years of outreach and expansion.

Dr. Blair has been used as a speaker at many national and state Sunday School conventions. Calvary Temple, an independent church, is respected for its total church educational program. The following principles are not original with Dr. Blair, but are those which have been observed in the church.

1. *As the Pastor Goes, So Go the People.* Dr. Blair believes the minister should give leadership to the total program of the church. He quotes John Mott, the missionary statesman, "Whenever the church has failed it has failed because of inadequate leadership."

Capable men have been hired to carry out the educational program. Reverend James Spillman, Director of Christian Education, is a main key in the leadership combination, along with the other full time ministers: Dave Koser, John McCahan, Wallace Pearson and Orval Terrell. The Reverend Mr. Spillman is the originator of the Alpha and Omega programs used by Success with Youth, Inc., Chicago.

Reverend Harvey Schroeder, Minister of Music, completes the

pastoral staff. Under his talented leadership the eighteen choir staff members co-ordinate approximately six hundred voices into the ten choirs. Pastor Schroeder conducts the Temple Voices and the Teen Choir.

Other administrative staff personnel include Roy S. Hudgins, Business Administrator, and Wendell Nance, Director of Development and Stewardship.

The driving leadership of Blair is the main contributing factor for the attendance growth. As you see him meet his people arriving at the front door on Sunday morning or feel his radiating personality from the pulpit, you are convinced he is the man God is using to build Calvary Temple.

Yet, Blair will not take the credit. He claims, "By and large our church is a staff-led church and could not possibly succeed without the valuable suggestions that have been made by our laymen."

Blair does not call Calvary Temple successful, at least by New Testament standards. He feels there is too much to do in God's sight to call it a successful church. When pressed for an answer to the key to success, at least in the eyes of men, Blair states, "I attribute the growth to a number of factors. The primary factor being the interest shown to each age level."

2. *The Whole Person.* Blair mentions another factor for the success of Calvary Temple. Says Blair, "We give attention to every age and endeavor to meet the needs of the whole person, spiritual, social, and physical." The whole person is ministered to by the whole church program.

No age is overlooked at Calvary Temple. Blair states, "Whether it is preschool or teenage, we try to give equal emphasis to the development of the individual." In Calvary Temple there is not only a class for the Young Single Adults, such as found in most large churches, but a class for older single adults (age fifty-five and above) named The Bible Explorers. This class was formerly called The Glowing Embers.

A glance at the weekly program will reveal a program for most every age and every person in the community. The greater Denver area is the parish for Calvary Temple, many of the members bypassing other evangelical churches on their way to church on Sunday morning.

The future plans of the church call for a Christian education campus with athletic field, gymnasium, swimming pool, tennis courts, and educational buildings, for each age level. Christ is to be at the center, and the total life of man will be reached, spiritual, mental, physical and emotional.

The present recreational program consists of basketball, softball, swimming, golf, bowling, skiing with the various age groups.

3. *The Visitation Program.* The organized program of outreach has varied throughout the years. Blair feels it is wise to keep a new challenge before the people. So he adds versatility and adaptation to the ministry of visitation. There are times when certain hand-picked laymen are involved in a thirteen week period. At other times the Sunday School classes or other educational agencies of the church are responsible for visitation. Also, assignments for visitation are sent through the mail.

In the "March to Sunday School in March" contest, laymen are active in canvassing, calling and census taking.

October is Enlargement Month. Sunday School teachers, church officers and group captains of classes visit in every home of the church during the month.

The full time staff members and pastors make over two hundred calls a week (not including hospital or sick calls). They are assigned divisional responsibilities, and assist in absentee and prospect visitation.

4. *The Promotion Program.* The promotion and advertisement program of the church is the responsibility of the executive members of the church staff. The church calendar is the starting point, and certain events are given emphasis. The church has secured professional help in regard to church newspapers, advertisement, brochures and other printed outreaches.

The Sunday morning service is broadcast over nine television stations in what is called the Rocky Mountain Empire. However, mail comes from a much larger area reflecting the popular acceptance of the program.

Sunday School contests, such as "Operation Andrew," spark attendance. Each class is given a percentage goal for growth and the total publicity means of the church are mobilized to "push" for the goal. The Harmonnaires had a 122 per cent growth and won first place in the contest.

The high schoolers had a 56 per cent increase with an average of 196 during the six weeks, compared to an average of 122 the previous year.

Blair said of this contest, "I have never seen so much participation on the part of so many." He mentioned a member, Wendell Nance, who walked the halls with a sandwich board encouraging attendance.

On the final Sunday, Easter, 3,844 attended Sunday School but greater satisfaction was the 108 decisions for salvation, 43 who came for baptism, and 110 coming for church membership. No one could convince Blair that Sunday School contests do not have their place.

Yet, contests are not a week to week occurrence at Calvary Temple. Blair has stated, "We do very little Sunday School promotion."

5. *Organization for Growth.* The thirty members of the full time staff — including business manager, secretaries, custodians — all reflect an efficient, organized team. Blair believes in organization and uses efficiency to the glory of God.

The church is a non-profit Colorado corporation with forty-five on the Board of Directors. According to Blair, "Policy has been set by a combination of ways. Often the recommendation has come through the pastor or a member of the staff, and at other times through the action of the official board.

The church is staff lead and even though each staff member has his delegated duties, each is responsible to Dr. Blair.

The Sunday School Superintendent is a layman who has served in this capacity for twenty-one years.

There is no Board of Christian Education. The usual decisions and duties in this area are the responsibility of the full time staff members.

6. *Up-to-date Teaching Techniques.* Even though Calvary Temple desires to enlarge its attendance, Blair feels the Sunday School should always be a first rate educational institution. He has stated his unwillingness to substitute quanitity for quality.

Team teaching is used in the lower grades. Use is made of many of the latest visual aids for learning.

But indoctrination is still considered central, for Blair states, "One of the guidelines of our Sunday School teachers is to give guidelines to biblical truth, to undergird and properly indoctrinate the student in matters of Christian doctrine."

The long range plan of a Christian education campus also has an educational methodology written into the blueprints. There will be an individual building for each age level, taking advantage of the teaching methodology involved. A library will be included in each building, giving opportunity for a three hour session on Sunday morning for children up through the sixth grade.

There are several programs of teacher training, but none so interesting as TTT (Temple Teachers Troup). A call was made for a militant group of people to teach Sunday School for three months in the summer and fall. Recruits were signed up army style in the church hallway for a "hitch" or "tour of duty." Potential teachers were encouraged to join the Lord's army to help bring victory.

7. *The Total Educational Program.* Calvary Temple has aimed at serving the whole person, and attempts to do so through the total educational program.

The Alpha and Omega youth programs are used in the Junior High and High School departments, respectively. The "O" House, a large home located next to the church, is used by the teen department for Sunday School and youth activities. Last spring eighty-eight graduating seniors left the Omega House to become a part of the College Department.

The College, Career and Military outreach has an enrollment of 250. The activities for this department are centered at Delta House, a large eleven-room estate on three acres including a swimming pool and tennis courts. This property is adjacent to the Omega House.

During the summer the youth program sponsored Christian Peace Corps, in which thirty-eight high schoolers were sent three thousand miles by bus to work in an orphanage in Ensenada, Mexico. The youth did spare jobs in the homes of church members at $1.50 per hour to finance the trip.

Pioneer Girls is an important club program that reaches the school age girl for Christ.

The total program includes a complete graded camping program for children and youth climaxing with a family camp. Vacation Bible School is an important summer outreach in June, with day camping later in the summer.

One-third of the financial income of the church is donated to foreign missions, with the church supporting wholly or in part 205 individuals in 75 families in 43 countries around the world.

8. *Reaching Out.* The church has a broad outreach. In recent

church newspapers such groups or films as the following were advertised as cooperating with Calvary Temple: the Billy Graham Evangelistic Association, Wycliff Bible Translations, The Spurrlows, Youth for Christ, World Vision, and the Navigators. Dr. Blair is on the regional board for the National Association of Evangelicals.

Calvary Temple cannot be identified with any one socio-economic sector of society, for the church draws people from all sections and segments of the city: doctors, attorneys, executives, laborers, and the poor. Even though the church is predominantly white, there are representative groups of blacks, Chinese and other minority groups in the congregation.

Calvary Temple has an exciting future, should the Lord tarry. The Christian education campus is a unique adventure for churches and the concept of "the whole man" is a revolutionary concept for evangelicals. Charles Blair is a young pastor (forty-eight years of age) in comparison to the other ministers in this study. Calvary Temple may blaze new trails out of the Sunday School apathy of the late 60's.

11

Factors Causing Growth
Based on the Church Program

Twelve years ago the Reverend Jerry Falwell began Thomas Road Baptist Church, and today it is listed among the ten largest Sunday Schools of America. There were perhaps many other churches founded at approximately the same time, yet they have not grown at the rate of Thomas Road Baptist Church, or perhaps haven't grown at all. Why?

The factors listed in this chapter relate to the church program, rather than the Sunday School. Of course the Sunday School and church program are vitally united in these churches but for sake of clarity, these two programs are separated. This chapter deals with factors causing church growth based on the church program. The items are not listed in order of importance, but are listed as they occurred on the questionnaire.

The total listing of the statistics are found in Chapter 14. Those data considered important to illustrate or validate the principles are listed. However, the reader will want to compare figures for a full understanding of each principle.

The statistics could have been divided into sections and placed with each principle in this chapter but this organization of material might not have been as profitable to the reader. It was felt that placing all of the statistics in one place, would enable the reader to compare and formulate principles of his own.

1. *Sunday School and Church Are One.* The Sunday School is considered the evangelistic outreach for the church and the church service is the place where the decisions for Christ are made. The ten largest Sunday Schools do not consider themselves as secondary to the church program, but part of a total outreach. The Sunday School and church program are vitally united.

Dr. Clate Risley, former Executive Secretary of the National

Sunday School Association said of Sunday School and church relations:

> Everybody that comes to Sunday School ought to stay for church. Everybody that comes to church ought to come early enough for Sunday School. There is a place for both, and if both are not interested in both, there is something wrong with both.

This statement reflects the attitude of the ten largest Sunday Schools.

The pastors in the ten largest Sunday Schools are vitally concerned with the life of the Sunday School. In most cases the Sunday School superintendent is directly responsible to the pastor. In the First Baptist Church of Hammond, Indiana, Dr. Hyles assumes the role of Sunday School superintendent. Stanley Bond of Akron Baptist Temple, even though a layman, has been Sunday School superintendent for thirty-five years since the founding of the church. Canton Baptist Temple and Temple Baptist Church of Detroit employ a full time Sunday School superintendent. But still, the pastor makes his personality felt in the Sunday School. Even though the Sunday School is run by laymen, it is not considered a layman's concern.

These churches rate the Sunday School as the most important outreach of Christian education, and in some churches the Sunday School overshadows the morning service. The pastors televise their Sunday School classes at Canton Baptist Temple and Akron Baptist Temple.

2. *Strong Pulpit Ministry.* The pulpit ministry of the ministers in the ten largest Sunday Schools seems to be authoritative. In this world of uncertainty and confusion, even in theological realms, the trumpet tones from these pulpits do not give an uncertain sound. These men believe that the Word of God always has been and always will be the answer to the basic needs of the human personality. These ministers are ardent, enthusiastic, unbiased Biblicists who believe that they have a relevant message for every man on earth. Within their own limitations of time, space and opportunity, these pastors will make every effort to communicate the message to the people in their own way. These men feel that literature, helps, films, pictures, are all good, but secondary to the major importance of giving out the Word of God. Some of the preachers are topical,

others are expository giving a running commentary of the Word of God, but all center upon the Bible.

The sermons tend to be Christo-centric. There is much preaching on the cross of Jesus Christ and the gospel to save men. These ministers do not give lip service to Christ as having the pre-eminence, but rather, strive to magnify the risen living Christ as a personal reality, a loving Saviour, an indwelling person, and the coming King of kings.

One of the ministers from the Baptist Bible Fellowship indicated what he regarded as the reason the men in the largest churches were successful; "While many pastors and churches in many denominations are lingering long over their jeremiads, lamenting the decline in interest and concern among the churches, the majority of our preachers, with mingled humility and zeal are pressing forward with vision and vitality." In a further comment, he stated, "Pastors who believe the Bible, ought to come down out of their ivory towers of socialiteism, or up out of the slough of despondency and discouragement, or off their plush upholstery and get out into the arena of life, going into the homes of people with the gospel, witnessing courageously and courteously in places of business, and dealing with people and their problems, giving them Christ as the Saviour and solution of their life."

This man went on to offer a conclusion, "A spirit filled, soul winning pastor, a dynamic nucleus of leadership inspiring zealous personal soul winners, will revolutionize any evangelical church in the world."

3. *The Length of Pastor's Service.* The average length of the pastor's tenure in the church is twenty-two years and one month among the ten largest Sunday Schools. Dr. Dallas Billington has the longest tenure, having been pastor of the church thirty-five years and Dr. Jack Hyles and Dr. Harold Fickett have the shortest tenure having been at their respective churches for only ten years. Perhaps the principle for building a large Sunday School is for a young minister to settle down in one church and do a constructive building program in the Sunday School over a period of years rather than candidating at other churches, trying to climb the rungs on the ladder of success to the largest church possible.

4. *Pastoral Leadership.* Five of the churches were either begun by the present pastor or the work was in its infancy when the pastor was called. They are the Akron Baptist Temple, Canton

Baptist Temple, Calvary Temple, Temple Baptist Church, and Thomas Road Baptist Church. In four of the other churches the church was not making notable progress and in some cases was even deteriorating: First Baptist Church, (Hammond), First Baptist Church, (Van Nuys), Highland Park Baptist Church and Landmark Baptist Temple. First Baptist Church, Dallas, seems to be the only church where the present pastor inherited a great work and continued the growth.

A criticism often heard of the top ten Sunday Schools is, What's going to happen to the work built upon a personality of a pastor when the pastor leaves? The answer is simply, "The pastor doesn't leave. He spends his whole life in one church." We can only speculate as to what will happen when some of these men go to be with God. "Suppose the work does go down in attendance," stated the Reverend Kenneth Mayers, Executive Secretary of the Sunday School of the Evangelical Free Church. "What's wrong with twenty-two years of stable growth, reaching multitudes of people, and building a solid work for God."

5. *Nine of the Ministers Are from the South.* Only one of the ministers in the ten churches comes from outside the South. Harold Henniger was born in Akron, Ohio, and grew up under the influence of Dallas Billington at Akron Baptist Temple. Later he went to Fort Worth and studied at the Baptist Bible Seminary. He went on to build a Sunday School based on the blueprint learned from Billington and J. Frank Norris, the late pastor of First Baptist Church in Fort Worth.

Six of the ministers and/or churches can trace the influence of J. Frank Norris upon their Sunday school organization (either first or second generation influence) and the pattern for structuring the Sunday School that was formulated under Norris can be seen in these six churches. (The church that Dr. Norris once pastored, and claimed to have the largest Sunday School in the world, now has approximately three hundred in attendance.)

Three of the men attended Southern Baptist Theological Seminary in Louisville (Criswell, Fickett and Roberson). Two of the men attended The Baptist Bible Seminary in Fort Worth. Three men are connected with the Baptist Bible College of Springfield, Missouri; Falwell as a graduate, Vick as president and Rawlings as vice-president. Three men did not have formal theological training.

6. *Evangelism.* Perhaps the greatest key to the success of the

ten largest Sunday Schools is their evangelistic zeal. Each of the ten largest Sunday Schools gives an evangelistic invitation at the end of the morning service, inviting people to come forward and receive Christ. (Many of them include church membership and baptism in the invitation.) The invitation is given both Sunday morning and Sunday evening, and the Highland Park Baptist Church, Chattanooga, and First Baptist Church, Dallas, give the invitation also on Wednesday evening. The ministers seem to be men of God with great trust in the power of God to convert sinners. They believe that God will work through their preaching for the conversion of the lost.

The invitation is the culmination of a week of evangelistic endeavors. Most of these churches have a strong visitation program during the week. Many of them require their Sunday School teachers to make evangelistic calls on prospects with a view of winning people to Jesus Christ. Most of these churches refer to these workers as "soul winners." When people are led to Jesus Christ, they are instructed to come forward during the invitation on Sunday morning.

When you are present in the main church services, you usually see a trained core of lay leaders ready to deal with those who come forward. Many times the "soul winners" come forward before the unsaved start coming so they may be ready to deal with the "seekers." This has given rise to the criticism that some of these churches, "prime the pump." That is, create a "bandwagon" mentality in the audience by getting their soul winners to come first, making it easy for the shy, timid sinner to come forward. However, not all of the ten churches have their counselors come forward first.

Several verses of the invitation hymn are sung in most of these churches. In a recent service, the author observed, three folks came forward at the end of the third stanza of the invitational hymn. The pastor stopped and asked every Christian to pray, "Our whole existence as a church is centered in this invitation, to save souls," stated the pastor. With all of the warmth possible, he asked any unsaved person who was not going to heaven to raise his hand. The minister indicated he would pray for those who raised their hand. Several hands were raised. The invitation hymn was sung again and eleven people responded. Three ladies in particular knelt at the altar and wept because of conviction of sin.

Some ministers might evaluate the ministers of the ten largest Sunday Schools as "being able to pull the net." Laymen evaluate these ministers as "men of God being used to win sinners to Jesus Christ."

The ministers of the ten largest Sunday Schools do not expect their people to do a job they are unwilling to perform. These ministers tend to be just as active as their members, witnessing for Jesus Christ and attempting to win the lost. This was evident when the author introduced himself to a converted Catholic one Sunday morning, only to find that she had been witnessed to the previous week by a minister as he checked out at the local A & P store.

The ministers (especially those belonging to the Baptist Bible Fellowship) of the ten largest Sunday Schools do not speak of evangelism as *witnessing*. Witnessing can be defined as a neutral term whereby we either *become* a witness through our life or *give* a witness by our testimony. This may simply be telling people what God has done for us, or what He is willing to do for them. The ministers tend to reject the term *witness* in favor of the term *soul winning*. The term soul winning indicates pressing for decisions, giving people the opportunity to accept or reject Jesus Christ. The people in these churches are exhorted to an "action" approach to evangelism, securing results in dealing with the lost.

In at least six of the churches, the author observed laymen walking up and down the aisle during the invitation asking unsaved people to go forward and receive Jesus Christ.

Also, evangelism is a strong theme in the Sunday School classes. One usually thinks of Sunday School as educational. Perhaps Jerry Falwell of Thomas Road Baptist Church best reflects the attitude of these churches, "I feel very strongly that Sunday School teachers should indoctrinate Biblical truths and not simply discuss the issues of Biblical truth." He went on to say, "We should teach for decisions." Dr. Fickett of Van Nuys disagreed, stating a discussion approach is used in their classes. The First Baptist Church of Dallas indicated they followed the emphasis of Nashville, the location of the Southern Baptist Publishing House.

The pastors of these ten largest Sunday Schools do not take a haphazard approach to evangelism. The visitation program is organized and Sunday School teachers are held accountable for their visitation. Dr. Harold Henniger of Canton Baptist Church indicated, "If you leave visitation up to the convenience of your folks, they won't do it." He is in the process of reorganizing his adult visitation program, knowing that the best intentions of men are often laid aside. He feels that those doing visitation should come to the church on Tuesday night, be assigned a specific responsibility (certain cards with names and addresses) and that these workers should be followed up to make certain that they have performed their visitation responsibility. Dr. Henniger went on to say, "The attendance of our Sunday School can be tied directly to the amount of visitation by our people."

Two churches in this study — Calvary Temple and Thomas Road Baptist Church — do not have an organized visitation program. However, both pastors agreed that the personal witnessing of their people accounted for the Sunday School growth.

Many years ago the author was a theological student in the city of Dallas, Texas. He had been married a year and was planning on a ministry in the Presbyterian church. He went to the First Baptist Church to hear Dr. Criswell preach. He filled out the visitor's card. During the next two weeks, eight calls were made to the home of the young theologian and his wife by members of the First Baptist Church. Though not a member of a Baptist denomination he decided to attend the church and learn church organization. "I felt those folks really wanted me to come to their church." Because of this experience he was later immersed and became a member of a Baptist church.

7. *Personal Salvation Is Primary; Social Action Is Secondary.* As you talk to the pastors of the ten largest Sunday Schools, their major burden is the winning of lost men and women to Jesus Christ. The culmination of a week of church activities is the invitation on Sunday, when the unconverted are invited to "walk the aisle" and receive Jesus Christ. These pastors do not use the invitation as a "technique" to get larger churches and Sunday Schools. The author believes these ministers are men of God with great personal integrity who have a burden to reach the lost. Because of this consuming passion, God honors their faith and the Holy Spirit works through their preaching to bring the lost under conviction and to salvation.

There is a tendency to criticize churches that emphasize evangelism, charging them with omitting the social implications of the gospel. However, a careful examination of the ten largest Sunday Schools and their social outreach would surprise the critics. First Baptist Church, Hammond, Indiana, has a rescue mission where meals are served to transients, a clothes storage depot in which clothing is provided to needy families, a barbershop where haircuts are supplied free, a Sunday afternoon hot lunch program where children from inner city areas are given a meal. Also, in an attempt to reach the neighborhood a Spanish speaking Sunday School and church service is held. Dr. Hyles states, "Our church does more social gospel work secondarily, than most liberal churches do primarily." He stated, "Our primary aim is to win souls; any social work we do is secondary."

Thomas Road Baptist Church, Lynchburg, Virginia, has a half way house for former prison inmates, Elim Home for Alcoholics, a city rescue mission. Highland Park Baptist Church of Chattanooga sponsors the Union Gospel Mission for the meals and lodging of transients. Last year, 2,181 campers (many from the innercity slum area) were given a free week at Camp Joy. Calvary Temple of Denver, Colorado, is constructing the Evangel Hospital in an humanitarian outreach into the city of Denver. Most of the churches provide classes for the deaf, emotionally retarded and special activities for senior citizens.

Of course, not all the churches listed have the same emphasis in social gospel implications, but there are enough instances of organized outreach into needy areas of community life, that one cannot make the general accusation that they are against the social gospel implications.

8. *Baptism.* Nine of the ten largest Sunday Schools are Baptist in conviction. All the Baptist churches require immersion for church membership. Dr. Falwell of Thomas Road Baptist Church perhaps reflected their attitude. "All candidates for membership must first be Scripturally baptized by immersion." Calvary Temple of Denver, the only non-Baptist church in the survey, baptizes by immersion, emphasizing it for new converts. But they do not require baptism for church membership.

Four of the churches in the study baptize immediately after a person accepts Christ. These are Akron Baptist Temple, First Baptist Church of Hammond, Highland Park Baptist Church of Chattanooga, and Landmark Baptist Church in Cincinnatti. This means that those who respond to an invitation on a Sunday morning are baptized immediately. Most of the other Baptist churches might not baptize a person during the same service in which they came forward, but might baptize a person during the evening service or the following Sunday.

Canton Baptist Temple is perhaps most cautious in its approach to baptism. Dr. Henniger, minister, states, "A member of our staff will visit each candidate for baptism before the person is actually immersed." One of the ministers was asked the question, "Don't you feel that in our modern sophisticated society, to ask a person to be placed under the water takes away from his dignity, hence attribute to the lack of growth in Baptist churches?" The pastor snapped at the question, answering, "A person who is willing to undergo this Scriptural ordinance is willing to take a greater stand for Christ than somebody who will allow a little water to be sprinkled on his head."

9. *Church Planting.* Evangelistic outreach is tied to local church ministry in the churches that were studied. The Reverend Mel Sabaka, Minister of Youth, Canton Baptist Temple, reflected the attitude of all ten when he states, "I'm against coffee house ministry, beach evangelism and any other type of so called evangelistic program that is not tied to the local church." Most of the ministers in these ten churches feel that expansion by evangelism will come best through starting indigenous local churches in outlying neighborhoods. Akron Baptist Temple claims to have started over two hundred churches since 1934 (this means financial support, purchase of property, loan of money to start building, or donation of song books to a church meeting in a store building or paying the salary of a man from an extension work). One of the churches it began with Canton Baptist Temple, which now is listed among the ten largest.

Highland Park Baptist Church in Chattanooga has forty-three missions, each of which, in Baptist tradition, is hoped will become a self-supporting Baptist church. There are thirteen churches in the city of Chattanooga that have been started by Highland Park Baptist Church that are no longer considered their mission chapels.

In the appendix of the book by McBeth, *First Baptist Church of Dallas*, there is a list of Baptist churches that at one time received help from the First Baptist Church, but no longer have an organic tie. The First Baptist Church of Dallas, sometimes jokingly referred to as "The Mother Church of the Southern Baptist Convention," at present has six mission churches.

There are many churches (not in the ten largest) who feel that they must limit the growth or attendance of the home church and start mission churches. In a recent visit to a church, the author heard, "We don't want to grow beyond four hundred in attendance."

Then the speaker added, "After reaching four hundred, we will limit our attendance and start building mission churches." Lyle Schaller feels that a church which limits its growth begins a program of self-destruction.

Dr. Lee Roberson of Highland Park Baptist Church of Chattanooga states, "A church grows greater by starting missions. The main church grows larger by giving of its people to start missions." Dr. Roberson feels that by sending members out to start churches and work in mission chapels, it will infuse the home church with enthusiasm and evangelism that cause both institutions to grow.

10. *Informal Services.* The churches in this study tend to have informal church services. One might think the church service has nothing to do with Sunday Schools. However, an analysis of the morning worship service should be made because people who attend the largest Sunday Schools also choose the church based on its worship services. The churches tend to have informal services with an "anti-liturgical" emphasis. There is warmth and acceptance, where each individual feels important. When Dr. Jack Hyles is welcoming guests in a Sunday morning service, you feel as though you are the only person out of the three thousand present. The pastor is able to communicate warmth to the people.

Of course, some of these churches are more ritualistic than others, while they all tend to be anti-formal. First Baptist Church of Van Nuys, California, has the doxology, call to worship and choral response to prayer someplace within the service. At the same time, when one visits Temple Baptist Church, Akron Baptist Temple, or Landmark Baptist Temple, you are not sure when the morning service actually begins. A song leader comes to the pulpit and leads in two or three songs while choir members walk to the choir loft from several places in the building. They do not file in. The worshippers do not have a printed order of service in their hands and the program is flexible according to the needs of the hour and the direction of the pastor. Announcements are important to inform the people of events in the church life. Also, people must be motivated to attend.

Jack Hyles specifically attacks the concept of the "worship hour." He recently stated, "We don't have liturgy. God lives everywhere So he instructed his people, 'Don't tiptoe in the auditorium and whisper. No! Grab the hand and say firmly, "God bless you." '" He went on to say, "I preach with all my heart because men are lost." He doesn't believe atmosphere and quiet help to worship God. He asks the question that screams for an answer, "What better way is there to worship God, than to have an evangelistic service in which the lost are saved?"

11. *Simple Organization.* The majority of the churches in this study believe that simple organization is one of the keys to their success. Dr. John Rawlings of Landmark Baptist Temple reflects this attitude when stating, "The way to grow corn is to get rid of the suckers." Rawlings referred to his boyhood on the farm and indicated that if the corn stalk had too many "extras," a good ear of corn could not be grown. In the same way, Rawlings indicated, if an organization has too many "committees" the end result of solid Christians will be dissipated. Rawlings went on to say that over-organization hurts church growth. He stated, "A church forms a committee to get a job done and the people originally appointed have the primary purpose of getting the job done." Then Rawlings elaborated, "Later, the people on the committee have as their primary function the keeping of the committee going, and its original purpose becomes secondary." He repeated the principle in homespun philosophy, "If a wagon has too much baggage, it can't roll; if a church has too much organization, it can't operate."

However, two of the churches in the ten largest indicate that organization is one of their keys to success. These are First Baptist Church of Dallas, and First Baptist Church of Van Nuys. Dr. Fickett of First Baptist Church, Van Nuys, writes, "On the human level, I would place organization and administration right at the top [among factors of success]. For example, we use the coordinator system which breaks a large organization down into small units with capable leadership at the head of each of these."

There seem to be two reasons for the contrasting opinion toward organization found in this study. The younger the church, the less the church is married to organization and dependent upon an efficient administration. The young church can grow on enthusiasm and leadership. As an illustration, those churches among the ten largest begun by the pastor tend to have little organization. At the same time, the older church with more stable history, tends to have a more complex organizational structure.

There is a second reason for the difference in the amount of organization. Those pastors who tend to have more charisma (this term means social leadership, and not pentecostal gifts) tend to have less organization and in contrast the pastors with less charisma tend to have more complex organizational structures. However, the observation of charisma and length of existence of the church will inter-relate as far as application of principles is concerned and are not mutually exclusive.

One final observation remains to be made concerning simple organization of these churches. They are obviously controlled or under the influence of the pastor who gives strong leadership. The pastor is the chief administrator both in the church, the Sunday School and/or the Christian education program of the church.

12. *Tithing.* As you view the multi-million dollar complex surrounding several of these churches, the question comes, "Who pays the bills?" Those ministers that have millionnaires within the congregation are quick to admit that smaller gifts rather than larger gifts are the backbone of their church. Each of the ten churches stresses tithing as the minimum obligation for the Christian. Dr. Lee Roberson claims that 75 per cent of his members at Highland Park Baptist Church are tithers. Dr. Dallas Billington of Akron Baptist Temple claims, "We only have one sermon on tithing per year — all year long." Recently, Dr. John Rawlings of Landmark Baptist Temple was receiving the offering and stated, "We expect the tithe of every Christian; that's 10 per cent from the gross income, before taxes." He went on to state, "If you wait to give 10 per cent after you've had income tax, social security, and union dues deducted from your income, you don't have much to give to God." Dr. Rawlings went on to indicate, "*Offerings* could be received also." This is giving over and above the tithe.

First Baptist Church of Dallas has an annual income almost twice that of other churches of similar size. Perhaps the reason for its financial success is the every member canvas conducted during the fall of the year. During this financial visitation program, each member is challenged to make a financial commitment to the church for the coming year. Tithes are stressed and each member is asked to sign a pledge card.

Dr. Vick of Temple Baptist Church states that one of the criteria for a successful minister is that "he must be a financier." By this, Dr. Vick indicates he must first of all be able to motivate his people to support the work financially; second, he must be able to arrange financing for the building campaigns and in the third place, he must be able to administer the financial income that is received.

Dr. Vick's first point seems to be most crucial. The successful minister must be able to motivate people to give money to God. Even though the ten churches stress tithing, one generalization may be said of the pastors – they are able to make laymen dig deep and give liberally.

13. *City-wide Ministry.* The average Protestant Church ministers to a local socio-economic neighborhood. One of the keys to the success of the ten churches is their ability to draw people from all areas of the city and from all walks of life. These ten churches transcend socio-cultural barriers. Schaller indicated, "The day is past when we can think in terms of a parish ministry." He mentioned this because of automobiles, expressways and mass media advertisement. Many people pass a church of like denomination on Sunday morning as they drive to their local church. Contributing to the decline of the local parish ministry is the mobility of the neighborhood, improvements in communication, and desire of individuals to attend the church of their cultural past rather than attending a church that is convenient in their neighborhood.

In spite of what Schaller has said, the average evangelical Protestant church tends to identify with one strata of society and one socio-economic neighborhood. Churches are usually tied to the neighborhood and the financial level of their congregation. But one of the strengths of the ten largest Sunday Schools is their, "freedom from neighborhood and socio-economic ties." The ten churches have a city wide ministry rather than a local neighborhood ministry. As such, these Sunday Schools attract all classes of society to their services.

Some of the ten churches were built on a blue collar clientele, such as, Akron Baptist Temple, Canton Baptist Temple, and Temple Baptist Church of Detroit. Many of these people were transient Southerners, who moved to the industrial Northern cities. However, several factors changed the church clientele. The passing of time, the original converts had children born in the northern cities, and the increased wage earnings of members brought a sophistication to these churches. As a result, these churches are no longer associated as lower class churches.

These ten churches have a warmth of emotionalism (without being highly emotional) and the freedom of an informal service. Many of the pastors who had predominantly lower class members are quick to point out they now have either professional men, business men, educators, or millionaires in their church. How are these people attracted to these churches? One answer is, "a city wide ministry." The rich, educated or professional (all considered upper class) from outside the neighborhood has the freedom to drive to the level and attract new members in an upper class neighborhood if the churches had emphasized a "local parish ministry." Many upper class individuals living in upper class neighborhoods, have lower class values and seek a church reflecting their value system.

Jack Hyles doesn't like the term "upper class." He feels that everyone who attends his church is upper class. But of course, he understands the socio-economic categorization of man. But at the same time, Hyles feels that we should not discriminate against a man for his low income. Dr. Vick stated, "God loves poor folks, because he made so many of them."

The uninformed minister should be warned against applying all of the principles found in the ten largest Sunday Schools, especially if he has a church located in a specific socio-economic neighborhood with a local neighborhood ministry. The principles of the ten largest Sunday Schools work because they are based on a city wide ministry.

14. *Total Church Program.* One of the contemporary criteria applied to successful Christian education is a "total church program," which includes camp, Vacation Bible School, mid-week club activities, and Sunday evening training hour.

However, when one examines the ten largest Sunday Schools, the lack of "total church program" is evident in most churches. Akron Baptist Temple does not have Vacation Bible school, nor does Highland Park Baptist Church and Temple Baptist Church. Mid-week club activities might be described as Pioneer Girls, Christian Service Brigade, Boy Scouts, or some similar programs. Canton Baptist Temple does not have mid-week club activities, neither does Highland Park Baptist Church, Temple Baptist Church, or Akron Baptist Temple.

At the same time the First Baptist Church of Dallas, Texas, and First Baptist Church of Van Nuys, California, have a complete program for the total man. (See chapter on First Baptist Church, Van Nuys for a description of a church that has a total church program for every age and every segment of the church family, yet is a growing Sunday School.) The program of the local church must be adapted to the needs of the individual.

Those churches that do not have club programs, have Sunday evening meetings of Scripture memory and Bible teaching. Also, some of the churches have similar programs during the week. When asked about a club program, Dr. Harold Henniger of Canton Baptist Temple stated, "I might consider it, but I would be afraid a club program might take away from the present staff of Sunday School teachers and workers who go visiting on Tuesday evening."

15. *An Emphasis on Separation of Members from Sinful Influences.* A common notion among evangelicals is that churches that have high standards of separation from sinful amusements and influences, will lose their attendance. In contrast, it is thought that churches with low standards of moral expectation from their members will have larger and growing attendance. Some mistakenly think that churches like "adult only" movies will attract great audiences if they give people what they want. This statement is not true. Each of the churches representing the ten largest in our nation have distinct, articulated, expressions of expectations from their members in daily practice. Members are expected to refrain from outward "worldly" amusements and practices. Akron Baptist Temple, the largest of the Sunday Schools, has such an extreme attitude toward separation that boys and girls are not allowed to swim together at their summer camp, but rather swim at different periods, separated by half an hour of time. Dr. Lee Roberson of Highland Park Baptist Church, Chattanooga was reading the newspaper when he saw the picture of one of his Sunday School teachers at a dance. He contacted the teacher and fired her from her teaching position. All the other churches to a relative degree, have the same concept of separation.

At the same time, the statement on separation from sinful activities should be qualified. The stand of Dr. Criswell at First Baptist Church, Dallas, on separation, would be considered extreme when related to other pastors in the Southern Baptist Convention. Dr. Criswell spoke from the pulpit concerning temperance laws in Dallas and has been known to say from the pulpit, "A Baptist should not have beer in his refrigerator." Yet some in the Baptist Bible Fellowship churches would consider Dr. Criswell too mild in separation. Especially is Dr. Criswell criticized in *The Baptist Bible Tribune* for continued support of the cooperative giving program among Southern Baptist churches, since it is regarded as an endorsement of the actions of the institutions. However, First Baptist Church, Dallas, supports only Southern Baptist institutions in Texas, not the entire Convention.

Also, the ten churches in the study do not cooperate with the local ministerial to any extent. They cooperate with denominational activities, and a few like Dr. Charles Blair, who serves on the Board of Directors for the National Association of Evangelists, cooperate with minister's groups of like persuasion. These churches do, however, have good relations with local ministerials (councils of churches).

16. *The Number of Full Time Paid Employees.* Years ago, the author heard a lecture in seminary that stated, "A church should employ a full time worker for every hundred people in its attendance." This generalization does not follow in the ten largest Sunday Schools. Some Sunday Schools fall far below the ratio, others are far above it. First Baptist Church in Dallas has eighty full time employees for its 4,500 average attendance. Akron Baptist Temple has twenty employees for its 5,700 average attendance. Of course, these employees include minister, associate and/or assistant ministers, educational workers, secretaries, custodians, full time printers, business managers, and cooks.

Perhaps one principle could be suggested. When there is work to be performed the churches are not reluctant to hire a person to perform the task. Most of the churches have at least one or more full time staff members involved in supervising the visitation program.

There seems to be a second principle, that the longer a church has been in existence and the more organized the internal administration of the church, the larger the church staff. This is reflected by Dr. Criswell's staff of First Baptist Church, Dallas, and Highland Park Baptist Church, Chattanooga. But, Thomas Road Baptist Church of Lynchburg, Virginia, contradicts this fact. It is the youngest church in the top ten yet has a large staff of thirty-eight workers.

17 *Parking.* Dr. John Rawlings of Landmark Baptist Temple feels that one of the factors for building a great church today is enough acreage to park cars. He indicated, "Look at your supermarkets and shopping centers. They wouldn't dare try to reach the

masses without providing parking." Dr. Rawlings has fifteen acres under blacktop for parking and room to expand his parking lot on the 160 acres of church property. This is one of the reasons why he feels his church can become the largest Sunday School in America.

Many of those who observe the rapid growth of Akron Baptist Temple as the largest Sunday School in the world, feel that Dr. Billington's vision of securing enough land for parking was one of the keys to the church's success. At present the church owns four-teen acres and has leased another twenty-one acres, which gives it unlimited expansion for parking. At present four thousand cars can park on its four different lots.

When Dr. Rawlings of Landmark Baptist Temple speaks to young pastors, he cautions, "Cheap ground can be costly." By this, he means that a smaller piece of property might be less expensive but in the long run would prohibit the church from growth. Re-cently a young man came by his church and thanked him for some advice. Five years ago, Rawlings told the young man to go to Florida, purchase ten acres of ground on an expressway and he could build a large Sunday School. The young man followed the advice of Rawlings, and within five years had a Sunday School with over six hundred in attendance.

18. *Emphasis on the Church As an Institution.* One of the most fascinating challenges was to determine the concept of the local church. What the ten churches said about their doctrine of church and what they practiced were at times widely separated.

The ten churches generally stress the local institution (organized church) as most important. The church was to be attended reg-ularly, to receive the tithes and receive the majority of attention by each member. If a Christian loved God, he expressed his love by faithfulness to the local church. The unsaved were to be brought to the church to be evangelized, and Christians were to attend the church to be "re-supplied" with motivation, training and direction — so they could go out (from the church) and win the lost. The church is the structure created at the sacrifice and investment of the people.

The church can be viewed as a group of *individuals* with empha-sis on the many or the church can be viewed as a *unit*. If you emphasize the individual, freedom, creativity and autonomy be-comes a dominant theme. If you view the church as a unit, discipline, purpose and duty become dominant patterns. The ten churches generally believe a church is a unit.

The ten Sunday Schools tend to feel the structure is more important than the parts. If you advance the organization (local church) the individual grows, for a strong church produces Christians who are dedicated in purpose, willing to sacrifice their personal feelings and ready to obey.

There is in America a growing ideology of the anti-institutional church. The individual is important. He must be well rounded, walking in God's grace and freedom, expressing the gifts and autonomy that is his. The way to expand attendance is to emphasize the individual. If there is a conflict, the local institution must sacrifice for the good of the members. Even though putting it this way may over-simplify the issue, there is no doubt that the ten churches emphasize the institution rather than the individual. One youth minister expected his young people to live up to the old proverb, "Soldiers and slaves ask no questions." He went on to state the youth of today were too spoiled, and must learn to yield to the demands of the group, to live a godly life. The large youth group reflected the success of his philosophy.

Is the individual an extension of the church or is the church the "sum total" of people? Obviously, the ten churches feel the church is important, and though none might admit it, the Christian is an extension of the church.

Conclusion

The factors in this chapter has sought to present those items that caused the church to grow. The questionnaire revealed a total of 520 items, but many principles were omitted in preparing this chapter. Principles that contribute to efficient church administration and sensible church management, but do not apply directly to Sunday School growth (thereby becoming a factor) were left off the list in this chapter.

The church worker who reads these pages should carefully consider applying all points. Try to approach these principles with an open mind. If the program is acceptable, you may want to buy the total package. If not, carefully evaluate your doctrine of ecclesiology, for one's doctrine of the church should determine the principles of administration and expansion. Simply stated, many ministers cannot accept the principles of this book because they hold a different doctrine of the church.

The hope of Sunday School is bright in these churches and as long as they continue their past program, we can expect growth in the future.

12

Factors Causing Growth
Based on the Sunday School Program

Sunday School growth is usually a trial and error affair. A new program is tried and if successful it is continued. If the new program fails — sometimes it is dropped, sometimes not.

Most Sunday Schools fail to grow in size because they fail to operate out of strategy or a planned program of outreach. Also, some strategy is misleading and will not produce growth. In order to grow, a Sunday School must have the right leader with the right strategy. The following factors were found to be those that produced growth in the ten largest Sunday Schools. The list is not in logical order, but follows the items on the questionnaires.

1. *Emphasis on Numbers.* In the ten largest Sunday Schools a consuming attention is given to numbers. One pastor told us, "Every Sunday morning when I get up, I am concerned whether it has snowed, rained, or we have beautiful weather. I get knots in my stomach worrying about how many we will have in Sunday School." Another of the pastors in the ten largest Sunday Schools was concerned about poor weather indicating, "Nineteen drops of water will keep twenty Baptists away from Sunday School."

Dr. Lee Roberson, was faced with the question of numbers. "Sure I'm interested in numbers," answered Dr. Roberson. "One is a number. Too often ministers say they are interested in quality and not quantity. One soul is a number and I am interested in reaching as many souls for Jesus as possible." Later, Dr. Roberson suggested that the churches who placed emphasis on numbers actually had a quality ministry.

Dr. Jack Hyles, First Baptist Church, Hammond, spoke to the issue of quality in Christians in a round table discussion for *Christian Life Magazine*, April, 1969, entitled "What Shall We Communicate?" He indicated that his people could be compared with

133

those from any other church and they would compare favorably. Hyles declared he tried to reach numbers because, "I believe every man and woman without Jesus Christ is going to Hell. I believe the flames of Hell are literal. And I believe Hell will last forever."

Dr. Vick of Temple Baptist Church justified his emphasis on numbers by pointing to the Scriptures. He pointed to the fact that Jesus had twelve disciples, later in the Book of Acts there were 120 people, next an emphasis was made on 3,000 conversions and finally over 5,000 souls were added to the church. Dr. Vick concluded, "I place emphasis on numbers because the Bible does."

Still another of the ministers of the ten largest Sunday Schools states, "God didn't call me to preach to empty pews. I do anything Scriptural to preach to multitudes."

Spurgeon told young ministers, "The man who isn't interested in numbers, won't have them."

The author heard many criticisms that these men were egotistical in their desire to reach large crowds. The author believes that the extreme emphasis on numbers by these pastors comes from a sincere motive to reach as many people for Jesus Christ in their life time. It is possible that pastors in smaller churches have confused secondary motives with primary factors. That is, they may have been more concerned with large Sunday Schools than reaching people for Christ. The ministers of the ten largest Sunday Schools have a primary desire to reach *large numbers* of lost people. This seems to be their primary motive. The secondary motive is to build a large Sunday School.

2. *Enrollment and Follow-up of Sunday School Pupils.* Some of the Sunday Schools plan to enroll more pupils, as part of a systematic outreach to expand the Sunday School. Dr. James Bryant, Minister of Evangelism, First Baptist Church, Dallas, stated, "Enrollment is more important than attendance. If enrollment goes up, attendance will automatically follow, but not vice versa." This has long been a Southern Baptist tradition. However, the largest Sunday School, Akron Baptist Temple, does not keep enrollment statistics. Some Sunday Schools have fewer enrolled than they have in actual attendance on a given Sunday.

Enrollment simply means the name of the pupil is on the roll book. In all the Sunday Schools, becoming a member of the Sunday School is an easy task. But the one significant point of enrollment is absentee follow-up. "Once we get a name on our rolls, the pupil feels an obligation to return," stated one pastor. "Then if the pupil is absent, we go after him."

What some churches call "prospect visitation" other churches call "absentee follow-up." Everyone of the ten churches had an extensive follow-up program. Even Calvary Temple and Thomas Road Baptist Church, who did not have a highly organized visitation program, did have a highly organized follow-up plan.

3. *Teacher-pupil Ratio.* One of the foundations of Sunday School laws has been, "Enrollment increases in proportion to workers at the ratio of ten to one."[1] This simply means a church usually has about ten times as many pupils as teachers. So absolute has been this law, that Barnette states, "A church by unusual efforts may attain more than this ratio for a time, but it is most difficult to maintain for a longer period than a few months a higher average than the ten to one ratio."[2]

However, most of the ten largest Sunday Schools do not reflect this rigid law. Many have a much lower ratio. The Canton Baptist Temple, which averages over 3,500 in Sunday School by this law, should have 350 teachers, but only has 210. Temple Baptist Church, Detroit, averaging 3,400 in Sunday School should have 340 teachers but in fact only has 200.

Most of the ten Sunday Schools have large youth and adult Sunday School classes. The large class is not a pragmatic solution to overcrowding, but a direct action based out of conviction that the "master teacher" will accomplish more than an inferior teacher in the small self-contained classroom.

4. *The Master Teacher and the Large Sunday School Class.* Most of the Sunday Schools have large youth and adult Sunday School classes, built around the capable teacher who can communicate to large classes. The conviction is that a teacher should be able to expand his class attendance according to the size of his capabilities. However, Barnette, defending the ten to one ratio attacks the large class. "There are a few large classes, but they are the exception, and as a rule are built around a strong personality rather than into a church program."[3] Many of the ten largest

---

[1] J. N. Barnette, *The Pull of the People* (Nashville: The Convention Press, 1956), p. 35.

[2] *Ibid.,* p. 36.

[3] *Ibid.,* p. 37.

churches believe in emphasizing the large adult class built around the strong personality, rather than into the church program. However, children's classes were always small (under ten in attendance).

5. *Divide and Multiply.* This traditional concept of growth is built on the ten to one model. Also, it is built on two other laws of Sunday School growth: "Classes reach their maximum growth in a few months after their beginning,"[4] and "new units grow faster, win more people to Christ and provide more workers."[5] The past theory has been to keep classes small for growth, and that dividing large classes, will cause both of the halves to grow. Rev. Mel Sabaka, Minister of Youth at Canton Baptist Temple, disagrees: "If a man can communicate effectively with one hundred pupils, why take ninety from him and give him only ten?" Then Sabaka adds a criticism against dividing: "Some of the ninety students may be given to an ineffective teacher, simply because you want to keep the class small." He would rather have the student in a large class with an effective teacher than a small class with an ineffective teacher. The consensus from the ten churches is that small classes do not automatically guarantee effective teaching, but the gifted individual (master teacher) can communicate whether he speaks to a large or small class.

Perhaps the largest class is Dr. Billington's adult Sunday School class in the church auditorium where an average of 2,200 come to listen to him teach the Word of God. This class is televised live throughout northern Ohio. At the end of the class, Dr. Billington gives an invitation and each Sunday there are responses for salvation, church membership or baptism. The class is much like a church service, and as a result many adults do not stay to the 11:00 o'clock hour.

The same pattern is followed in Canton Baptist Temple where Dr. Harold Henniger teaches a Sunday School class of 1,500. The adult class at Landmark Baptist Temple averages 1,100 in attendance.

Temple Baptist Church in Detroit has seven large adult classes ranging in attendance from 150 to 500. Though not as large as the auditorium classes in the other churches, these are large Sunday

---

[4]*Ibid.*, p. 37.
[5]*Ibid.*, p. 38.

School classes, taught by full time staff members, who are responsible for visiting their class members during the week. Volunteer workers from these classes help in visitation, going out and inviting visitors to "their" Sunday School class. The churches following this system have keen competition among classes, building a strong Sunday School class identity. Some of the Sunday School classes are publishing their own weekly newspaper.

Some of the large Sunday School classes have caused problems for the church. (See the chapter on First Baptist Church, Dallas.) But for the most part, they provide continued growth to the total Sunday School attendance.

6. *The Pastor As Sunday School Teacher.* Most of the pastors in the ten churches teach a Sunday School class. While pastors in smaller churches, feel they need to prepare themselves spiritually for the morning message, the pastors in the large churches are enthusiastic supporters of Sunday School, teaching a class themselves. According to Dr. Hyles, "Why shouldn't the pastor, who is usually the best teacher in the church, teach a Sunday School class? Why should he hide his talent under a bucket?" This is an interesting question that demands an answer, especially of pastors in young struggling churches.

7. *Sunday School Literature.* Seven of the ten largest Sunday Schools write and publish all or most of their own literature. Of the publishers, Southern Baptist Publications, supplies literature to two churches; Gospel Light supplies one church; Scripture Press supplies a part of the material at two churches; and Baptist Publications, Denver, Colorado supplies part of the literature for two churches.

Some of the churches rely heavily on the publishers. Akron Baptist Temple writes its own material only in the adult departments. In the cradle roll through the youth divisions, the teachers have quarterlies from Baptist Publications, Denver Colorado, but they do not distribute quarterlies to pupils. Canton Baptist Temple prints an outline from a central theme from the Word of God, but they use Baptist Publications with their toddlers and Scripture Press Publications with the beginners. Highland Park Baptist Church of Chattanooga, Tennessee, prints its own outline for distribution to its teachers, but uses Scripture Press through the primary department.

The churches that write and print their own Sunday School

outline, do so out of conviction. It is not a technique to save money. Dr. Hyles feels a publishing house does not know the needs of his pupils as he does; therefore he writes his own material. Dr. Vick of Temple Baptist Church, Detroit, believes the introduction of Sunday School literature into a church is one of the first steps leading to liberalism.

One of the keys to the success of the Sunday School is not the fact that the church writes and prints its own curriculum, but rather that the pastor or staff member teaches the material to the teachers at the Wednesday night teacher's meeting. Many of the lay teachers follow the pattern set by the minister. Dr. Hyles feels, "If I apply the Word of God to my pupils, they will teach the Word of God out of conviction when they go into their classes."

The Sunday School lessons of the late 1800's were taught in just such a fashion. In those days there were no central publishing houses to supply curriculum. As a result, the pastor or Sunday School superintendent provided an outline of the lesson, then instructed the teachers in the content and methodology. With the birth of the publishing house, and expansion of reading material the old format was dropped.

One teacher from Temple Baptist Church indicated, "I wouldn't miss teacher's meeting for anything. It saves me about two hours of preparation and I become a better teacher for having heard the pastor teach the lesson."

A criticism against "teach the teachers" approach is that a stream can rise no higher than its source. The Sunday School teacher, it is feared, will mimic the faults of the minister. If a minister or person who writes the Sunday School curriculum is narrow, goes off on a tangent, or is misinformed, the whole church will be mislead. This is a valid criticism and must be faced by those preparing curriculum whether at the local church or the publishing house.

Some pastors may read this book and decide the way to success is "throwing the curriculum out of the Sunday School." This is fallacious thinking. First of all, the men who are pastors of these churches are brilliant, gifted men. The very fact a pastor is in a small church may show his lack of capacity to do many things. Second, it is not the lack of literature that has led to successful churches, but the pastor's ability to teach the lesson on Wednesday evening that seems to be the key to success. A pastor should not drop literature from his Sunday School unless he is willing to take on a much larger work load.

A third argument against eliminating literature, is the area of application. Literature that is prepared by a team of specialists can take advantage of psychology, the latest teaching techniques and the fruits of curriculum study. The average pastor cannot possibly know all of the needs of his children's department as well as those of high school pupils. Sunday School publishers argue that a full time person, trained to meet the needs of an age level with theological, psychological and education training, should produce Sunday School literature.

Dr. Hyles has gotten around the problem of application by having the teachers attend a departmental meeting in which a staff member demonstrates how to implement the lesson to that particular age level.

8. *Weekly Sunday School Teacher's Meeting.* Seven of the ten largest churches have a weekly Sunday School teacher's meeting at which a large percentage of the active teaching staff is present. They report 70 to 80 per cent attendance at a weekly Sunday School teacher's meeting. The success of the Sunday School is not because the teachers come weekly, but because of the educational activities that go on at these meetings. These Sunday Schools do not purchase published Sunday School curriculum from a publishing house but rather write their own material. At the weekly teacher's meeting, the pastor or one of his assistants instruct Sunday School teachers in the lesson they are to give the following Sunday. Dr. Lee Roberson of Chattanooga feels, "If the Word of God is applied to the heart of the teacher with fire and enthusiasm, he in turn can become a better teacher on Sunday morning."

Dr. Jack Hyles of First Baptist Church divides his Sunday School teachers meeting into three sections. The first twenty minutes is given to an actual teaching of the lesson. He covers the lesson in a verse by verse explanation. The second twenty minutes is devoted to departmental meetings where a staff member demonstrates to teachers how the material is to be taught to the specific age group. Hyles sets aside the final twenty minutes for "promotion and motivation." During this time period he "informs and inspires" his teachers concerning coming promotions, contests and programs within the Sunday School. He states that if a Sunday School teacher is motivated, he will study, perform and visit. At the same time, Hyles indicated, "Teachers who are fully trained in the traditional sense (have a knowledge of their job requirements) do not always perform the requirements." Hyles went on to state, "If I get a man motivated, the academics and training takes care of itself."

9. *The Board of Christian Education.* Contrary to popular expectation, none of the churches in the study has a Board of Christian Education. One would expect that since so much is said about a Board of Christian Education at Sunday School conventions, that these churches would be examplary. The program of Christian education is under the direction of the full time staff member, the full time Sunday School superintendent, or the pastor. Perhaps Dr. Harold Fickett of First Baptist Church, Van Nuys, reflected the attitude of the churches, "We do not have a Board of Christian Education to supervise Sunday School. Our Christian education staff does that." His church did not have a Sunday School superintendent, but as he indicated, "Paid coordinators at the head of each division in the Sunday School perform the capacity of a lay superintendent."

The author asked Dr. Dallas Billington of Akron Baptist Temple why he did not have a Board of Christian Education. His answer was simple, "You tell me the duty of a Board of Christian Education, and I'll tell you why I don't have one."[6]

"The first duty of a Board of Christian Education is to determine educational policy."

To which he answered, "I do that."

"The second duty of a Board of Christian Education is to appoint educational personnel."

"I do that," stated Billington.

"The third duty of a Board of Christian Education is to evaluate and select the Christian education curriculum."

"I do that," stated Billington.

"A fourth duty of a Board of Christian Education is to plan the educational program of the year."

"I do that with my staff," stated Billington.

"The fifth duty of a Board of Christian Education is to formulate and adopt a budget for the educational program of the church."

---

[6]The author believes the church educational program in an average size church should be under a Board of Christian Education and has a forthcoming book to be shortly released, *How to Organize a Board of Christian Education.* However, the author feels larger churches should follow the pattern suggested above.

"I do that with the staff," stated Billington.

"The sixth reason for a Board of Christian Education is to evaluate the qualifications, hire the personnel for the Christian education program and to direct their activities."

"And I do that too," stated Billington.

Billington went on to state, "We don't need a Board of Christian Education. They only slow down the work of the church." Billington feels that democracy is not correctly understood. And he especially disagrees with those who call a committee form of church government, Biblical. Billington feels the New Testament teaches that leadership comes through the man of God and that Scriptural churches are led by men rather than committees.

10. *Goal Setting.* The ten largest churches generally set standards (expectations in attendance) for classes, departments and units within their Sunday School. Recently the following expectations were published by the First Baptist Church of Van Nuys. In the month of March, 1969, they attempted to reach an average attendance of 3,333 each Sunday. Each department was given the following expectations.

MARCH TO SUNDAY SCOOL IN MARCH 1969

We've set our attendance goals —

Division	Goal	March 2	March 9
Nursery	373	391	390
Beginner	290	260	270
Primary	380	430	416
Junior	470	484	520
Junior High	400	378	388
Senior High	290	342	294
CCC/R'20	240	260	249
Adult	890	918	947
Totals	3,333	3,463	3,474

A list of printed attendance expectations places responsibility for growth on the shoulders of those who are involved. A department that falls below expectations is rebuked, hence providing motivation for harder work on the following Sundays. The human motivation of "approval in the eyes of one's peers" is a great incentive for more diligent work.

11. *Promotion.* The churches in the top ten are unashamed of their programs, and are bold in their promotion and advertisement campaigns. In a printed questionnaire, each was asked to indicate what was their most successful promotion technique. *Each* of the churches indicated, visitation — house to house. However, the ten largest churches spend vast amounts of money in printed posters, handbills, newspapers, and other printed media. Each of the ten ran a large advertisement in the Saturday newspaper announcing the Sunday services.

Rewards play an important role in the promotion by some churches. Prizes or incentive gifts are given to those who attend. First Baptist Church, Hammond, gave away charms for a bracelet and Landmark Baptist Temple gave "Burger Chef" hamburgers to all those who rode the bus. The list of rewards used to entice pupils to Sunday School could be lengthened. But, at the same time, several of the churches do not use these techniques, indicating that their only motivation for outreach is evangelistic soul winning.

12. *Sunday School Contests.* Sunday School contests are very similar to promotion techniques. Some Sunday Schools will use contests, others will not. First Baptist Church, Hammond offered three free trips to the Holy Land for those bringing the most persons to Sunday School during a thirteen week period. The lady who won the prize brought 976 people during the contest. At the same time, other churches in the study would not conduct a church wide Sunday School contest. Some of the churches stay clear of contests, feeling that it cheapens the gospel. Others refuse to use contest because external motivation does not bring visitors to their church. Those churches that do not use a church wide contest, however, would allow an individual Sunday School class or department to run attendance contests.

The author was quite surprised at the small number of contests conducted in the ten churches. He had expected to see a large number of contests to attract attendance.

Jack Hyles was asked why he used Sunday School contests. "I'll do anything to get people into my church so I can preach the gospel to them." He went on to explain that the average person does not come to church today simply because the building is there. But people come because another person has invited them. "So I give my people an extra incentive to invite the lost to church." Hyles went on to state, "I don't care what the motive is for bringing lost people to church. A man can invite the unsaved to church for the glory of God or for a prize — just so long as the lost come." But he was quick to add, "I would wish that all Christians everywhere would bring the lost to church to glorify God, but I know they won't do it."

13. *Sunday School Busing*. Perhaps one of the controversial areas in the ten largest Sunday Schools is the attitude they have toward Sunday School busing. The Sunday School bus is used as an evangelistic tool to reach people for Christ.

Landmark Baptist Temple has the largest fleet of buses with seventy buses and routes spreading out over the greater Cincinnati area every Sunday morning. First Baptist Church of Hammond, Indiana, has the second largest fleet with sixty-five, one of them going as far as the Great Lakes Naval Training Station, eighty miles away every Sunday morning.

The Thomas Road Baptist Church indicated, "We're just beginning our bus ministry emphasis. At present we are running seventeen buses and bring in about seven hundred pupils per Sunday. We plan to enlarge to thirty buses this year with twelve hundred weekly riders."

At the same time, some of the ten Sunday Schools are de-emphasizing or do not use Sunday School buses. Years ago, the Akron Baptist Temple ran approximately forty buses throughout the greater Akron area, but when cost went up and their clientele changed, Sunday School busing was gradually phased out. Today, they have seven buses bringing in approximately 220 each week. Most of these buses are for older folks and children whose parents do not come. First Baptist Church of Dallas uses buses only in its inner city missions and chapel outreach but does not bring any pupils to the downtown church, except the children from Baptist Children's Home. However, the home furnishes the bus.

The First Baptist Church of Van Nuys has eight buses but none of them are used for Sunday School outreach. The buses are used for recreation, the day school and social activities. Calvary Temple of Denver has three shuttle buses connecting with city bus routes and brings approximately eighty to each service.

Dr. John Rawlings has the largest fleet of Sunday School buses and said of Canton Baptist Temple, "They don't put much emphasis on Sunday School buses. If Canton Baptist Church would invest as much energy on Sunday School buses as we do, they could be the largest Sunday School in the world." But Henniger does not want to go into an expanded program of Sunday School busing, feeling you cannot build a stable program on people who are bused to church.

Sunday School busing can give a false illusion of having many more people in church than are actually stable Sunday School pupils. It is easy to add a large attendance quickly through busing (see February, *Christian Life Magazine*, "Bus Service Puts Sunday School on Road"). But on the other hand, Sunday School busing can be an evangelistic outreach to reach into new neighborhoods and homes, bringing people under the sound of the gospel.

One of the chief criticisms of Sunday School busing ministries realize this, but nevertheless, use their buses to reach children and hence, sometimes whole families for Jesus Christ.

A second criticism of Sunday School busing is that they are most effective in inner city or slum neighborhoods. Dr. Jack Hyles deals with this problem in his church manual.[7] He first suggests eight areas from which to recruit pupils to ride the bus: (1) a housing project, (2) an apartment house area, (3) a trailer court, (4) an area cut off from the community, (5) a poor area, (6) schools or homes, (7) another town, and (8) country roads. Hyles deals with five areas of problems in a busing ministry. Three of these center around children from poor areas: (1) delinquent children, (2) misbehaviour in the services, and (3) criticism by members. This last point deals with children from a poor section of town. In a story Dr. Hyles tells of a well-to-do member who came to him and said, "Pastor, what are we going to do with all these little bus kids?"

"I don't know what you are going to do with them, but I'm going to love them," stated Hyles.

Then the member said, "If they stay, I leave."

To this he added a climax, "The bus children stayed and he left. We felt we got the best of the deal."

Even though children from poor families are easy to reach, Landmark Baptist Church has put its emphasis on middle class neighborhoods. Of their seventy buses, most of them cover the suburbs of Cincinatti, bringing in middle class children to the church.

---

[7]Jack Hyles, *The Church Manual* (Murfreesboro, Tenn.: Sword of the Lord Publishers, 1968), p. 157-66.

A third criticism of Sunday School busing is the high dropout rate of turnover in attendance of those riding the bus. The charge is that those who will ride the bus are not as stable or dependable; hence, there must be constant pressure to get new people to fill the seats on the bus. Dr. Jack Hyles answered this argument, "Sure, a lot of people from the bus ministry make decisions and never come back." He went on to say, "Suppose one man made a decision for Christ and stuck with the church and ten men made some type of decision and never came back? I'll go to that expense to get the one decision because every soul is precious in God's sight."

13

Methods of Research

This book began in the spring of 1968 when a student at Trinity Evangelical Divinity School questioned me as to which church was larger, First Baptist Church of Dallas, Texas, or First Baptist Church of Hammond, Indiana.

The author is also Sunday School editor of *Christian Life Magazine* so he determined to search out the ten largest Sunday Schools for an article in the magazine.

The author wrote to the Sunday School secretary of forty-two different denominations, asking for a list of the largest Sunday Schools in their denomination. To this list were added churches suggested by The National Sunday School Association, *The Yearbook of American Churches*, and the files of *Christian Life Magazine*. The executive secretaries of area Sunday School associations were written, asking for their awareness of Sunday Schools with large attendance in their area. After the list was completed, each Sunday School was written and asked to state their average attendance for the past twelve months. From these responses, a listing of the ten largest Sunday Schools in America was published. (The article appeared in September 1968. In spite of careful checking of figures, there were a few oversights that came to light in the following months.)

The author has carefully traced out each suggestion given to him and is not aware of any Sunday School with an average attendance high enough to place it within the ten largest in the United States.

By the term *largest* we mean the ability of the Sunday School to secure the attendance of more people on a sustained average when compared to other churches that are unable to sustain a high average.

The author has taken a case study approach in analyzing the ten largest Sunday Schools in America. He has concerned himself with (1) a descriptive study of the Sunday School, (2) a historical research into the past of the Sunday School, and (3) an examination of causal relationships to determine what factors the churches have in common that have brought about their high attendance.

Four questionnaires were used to gather facts from each church. The questionnaires were as follows. (1) The first was a factual questionnaire to gather basic data on the churches in the study (a six page instrument with 242 questions). (2) The second was an evaluative questionnaire, asking for a subjective effectiveness of each of the previous 242 questions. The first two questionnaires were sent simultaneously. (3) A more sophisticated questionnaire was constructed after the personal visit was made to the churches. This questionnaire attempted to compare factors that were evidently influencing the attendance of these churches. (4) A personal letter was written to each pastor in which he answered questions relating to his role in Sunday School growth.

Thirteen churches were studied, of which three were eventually dropped from the list because of their insufficient average attendance.

Of the ten churches in this study, seven were actually visited by the author. The author appreciates the patience of the pastors in these churches in answering questions, answering mail, and answering long distance phone calls. One minister said jokingly, "You ask more questions than a jealous wife."

The following criteria to guide in the case study was set by Carter V. Good and Douglas E. Scates, *Methods of Research* (New York: Appleton-Century-Crofts, Inc., 1954). This is an accepted text in research. The authors base their principles for case study upon the work done by Ralph W. Tyler in 1935.[1] The author accepts these criteria for case studies in the investigation of the ten largest Sunday Schools in the United States.[2]

1. *Must Concern Itself with Worthwhile Objectives.* Here Good and Scates indicate that discovery of major generalizations that are based on microscopic or partial evidence are invalid to inter-

---

[1]Ralph W. Tyler, "Characteristics of a Satisfactory Diagnosis," *Educational Diagnosis*, thirty-fourth Yearbook of the National Society for the Study of Education (Bloomington, Illinois: Public School Publishing Co., 1935), chapter 6.

[2]Carter V. Good and Douglas E. Scates, *Methods of Research* (New York: Appleton-Century-Crofts, Inc., 1954), p. 743.

pret new principles coming to the observer's attention. The author has tried to ask questions that have been basic in the formulation of principles that have caused Sunday Schools to grow. Some data was rejected because it was so minute in scope as to have little determination on attendance growth.

2. *Must Provide Valid Evidence of Strengths and Weaknesses Related to the Objectives.* If research is to be valid, it must consider all of the data and not approach conclusions with preconceived ideas. The ten largest churches have many strengths. But at the same time, they have many weaknesses. As has been noted elsewhere, the author does not recommend that all of the principles found in the ten largest Sunday Schools should be applied to every church situation, nor does the author feel that all of the principles followed by the ten largest Sunday Schools are necessarily Biblical. Some of the principles are "successful" because they are pragmatic, but not necessarily founded upon Biblical principles.

3. *Must Be Reasonably Objective to Permit Other Competent Investigators to Reach Similar Conclusions in Employing the Same Diagnostic Techniques.* The author is not aware of any study of principles of enlargement in Sunday Schools that have been systematically made on a laboratory basis. If an investigation of the ten largest churches has been made on an objective basis by any other researchers, it is not known to the author. However, he feels that future researchers interested in church process could interview the same ten churches and arrive at similar conclusions.

4. *Must Be Reliable, So That Repeated Diagnosis of Other Samples from the Same Learners Will Give Similar Results.* Good and Scates indicate that if the same tests or case studies were applied to other situations, the same results would be found. This principle would not apply to this study, because we have observed the ten largest Sunday Schools, which eliminates all other churches. If this study were applied to the ten largest churches of one denomination, the findings might be different because the ten largest churches of one denomintation might be substantially smaller in number than the ten largest Sunday Schools in the United States. However, if the ten largest churches on an interdenominational basis were taken in one section of the country, the findings might be similar in nature.

The author feels there are many areas of research available for the diligent student within the ten largest Sunday Schools. However, if in the future different measuring instruments were applied, the findings would be similar.

5. *Must Be Carried to a Satisfactory Level of Specificity.* In this study, over 520 items of specific data from each church have been gathered, analyzed and compared. Some of these items have been summarized by the observer, such as an attitude toward separation from sinful influence, an attitude toward evangelism, and summarization of the promotion techniques used by a church. At the same time, some items have been recorded exactly as reported by the Sunday School, such as average attendance, enrollment, total income for 1968, number of classes, and name of Sunday School publisher, etc. It is felt that the data presented is specific enough to lead to conclusions.

6. *Must Provide Comparable Data: Measurement of Progress at Intervals Requires Equivalent Test Forms of Procedures Adequately Standardized and Controlled.* The author has asked the same questions of all churches, using a battery of four tests with each Sunday School. The author has demanded certain standards for the application of data. Some churches include chapel attendance in with the main church attendance, other churches do not count the chapel attendance. Where this variation takes place, the author has noted the fact with an asterisk (*). Some churches have counted the home department (adults visited in the home because they are unable to attend church) as part of the Sunday School attendance. The author has indicated that home departments should not be counted. Other data was controlled so that churches were comparing measurable data rather than a comparison of apples and oranges.

7. *Must Provide Sufficient Data for Diagnostic Purposes.* The 520 items of data received are sufficient to give general principles on which Sunday School attendances have been built. However, the author is aware that an indepth study could be made from each one of these 520 items, each providing a thesis topic for some graduate student in a theological institution.

8. *Must Be Comprehensive or Complete.* At this point, Good and Scates indicate that the overall picture must be attained if specific principles are to be made. The author feels that the strength of such a study lies in the overall picture secured from each of the ten largest Sunday Schools.

9. *Must Be Appropriate to the Desired Program of Instruction.* Good and Scates indicate that any type of investigation involves highly individual rivalry or anti-social motivation would bring to question the end results. The author has no "ax to grind" with the ten largest Sunday Schools. Nor did he feel a rivalry with the top ten Sunday Schools on any basis. The author did receive a number of criticisms from Christian Education authorities who prejudged the ten largest Sunday Schools, saying, "They place such emphasis on numbers they can't have good educational quality." The author feels that if such Christian education authorities had attempted the study their principles could be questioned, in as much as they might have subjective motives in examining the data. Good and Scates also indicate excessive introspection may have an undesirable psychological emotional or social effect upon the conclusions. The author is not aware of any such introspective motives in his life. He feels that many struggling Sunday Schools are applying principles that will not, in fact, help the Sunday School grow. Some of the principles taught in Sunday School conventions and Christian education are contrary to those used by the ten largest Sunday Schools. These principles may keep a Sunday School from expansion in attendance.

10. *Must Be Practical in Terms of the Condition, Time, Personnel, Equipment and Funds Available.* The author realizes the weakness of this study. First of all, he was the only researcher-observer (which tends to give consistency of reporting of facts, but also limits the total observation of one church). A second limitation was the lack of time and finances for this study. The vast number of "factors" to consider began to swell the project so that a decision had to be made to limit the study. Enough data was gathered to make the study valid, yet enough data remains uncovered to make a doctoral dissertation.

11. *Must Be Conducted by Adequately Trained Students of Diagnosis.* Good and Scates indicate, "Such technically trained persons are to be found among teachers, supervisors, and administrators in the field where their efforts supplement with increasing effectiveness the work of clinics, laboratories, research agencies and psychological and educational specialists."[3]

---

[3]*Ibid.*

14

Statistics of America's
Ten Largest Sunday Schools

	Akron Baptist Temple Akron, Ohio	Highland Park Baptist Church Chattanooga, Tennessee	First Baptist Church Dallas, Texas	First Baptist Church Hammond, Indiana	Canton Baptist Temple Canton, Ohio
Minister	Dr. Dallas Billington	Dr. Lee Roberson	Dr. W. A. Criswell	Dr. Jack Hyles	Dr. Harold Henninger
Age of Minister	66	59	60	44	44
How long pastor has been in present church	1934/35 years	1942/27 years	1944/25 years	1959/10 years	1947/23 years
Education School		A.B. University of Louisville. Southern Baptist Seminary. LLD — Bob Jones University	B.A. Baylor PhD Southern Baptist Seminary	B.D. Southwestern Baptist Seminary D.D. Bob Jones Seminary	Baptist Bible Seminary, Fort Worth, Texas. D.D. Bob Jones University
Sunday School Attendance, 9-1-68 to 3-1-69. Please be exact.	5,762	4,821	4,731	3,978	3,581
Total Enrollment	Don't keep this statistic	7,627	8,655	7,119	5,025
Number of Sunday school teachers (not substitutes).	506	388	497	334	810
Number on volunteer staff of Sunday school	800+		945	412	80
Number of full time paid staff, including secretaries, janitors, business assistant	20	41	80	18	13
Building value. Today's estimated value. Include property.	$7,000,000	$1,700,000	$8,000,000	$2,500,000	$1,500,000
Acreage attached to church.	14 owned 21 leased	110 acres. Buildings are being used (many of these belong to Tenn. Temple school	0	0	12
Number of off-street parking spaces provided by church.	4,000+	Parking for 750 cars.	1,100		1,400
Seating capacity in sanctuary	2,500	3,400 in main auditorium. Two additional auditoriums used plus 43 chapels.	2,495	2,000	2,278
Educational space (list in square floor footage).	125,000		250,000	115,000	111,000
Sunday school publisher. If you use more than one please indicate or if you use a publisher for only part of Sunday school please indicate.	Write and print our own Adults. Baptist Publication Birth through Youth. Teachers have quarterlies but not pupils.	Write their own. Print a Sunday school outline in the weekly church paper. Scripture Press thru Primary Department.	Southern Baptist Publications.	Write and print their own outline. A full time director of literature writes all Sunday school material.	Teach only the Bible. Print an outline of a central theme from the Word of God. Use Baptist Publications with Toddlers. Scripture Press — Beginners.

Landmark Baptist Temple Cincinnati, Ohio	Temple Baptist Church Detroit, Mich.	First Baptist Church Van Nuys, Calif.	Thomas Road Baptist Church Lynchburg, Virginia	Calvary Temple Denver, Colorado
Dr. John Rawlings	Dr. G. B. Vick	Dr. H. Fickett	Dr. Jerry Falwell	Dr. Charles Blair
55	68	51	35	48
1951/15 years	1935/33 years	1959/10 years	1956/12½ years	1947/23 years
Bible Baptist Seminary, Ft. Worth.	Never ordained	Th.D. Eastern Baptist 1950. D.D. Wheaton, 1957	Lynchburg College, 2 years. Baptist Bible College, ThG. Tennessee Temple and Seminary, D.D.	
3,540		2,847/week	2,640	2,453
Don't keep	6,500	4,800	5,050	3,052
350	235	400	118	206
540	285	650	212	332
32	20	30	38	30
$5,000,000	$4,000,000	$5,500,000	$1,500,000 (not including youth camp — Alcoholic home, etc.) Just breaking ground for 1 million plus bldgs.	$2,000,000
160	16	20	18	29
16 acres paved for parking	1,300	940 paved 400 unpaved	500 autos (to be greatly enlarged)	1,000
2,500 (3 youth services simultaneously)	4,800	2,000	1,200 (only adults attend in sanctuary. Youth and children have own sanctuary)	2,300
115,000	178,000		65,000 — 44,000 additional under construction. New sanctuary will seat 3,000 plus.	Approx. 140,000 plus using two cafeterias nearby.
Write their own. H. Rawlings writes lessons. Flannelgraph used from several companies.	Write their own. Take home papers for primary.	Southern Baptist Publications and Scripture Press.	Write their own.	Gospel Light Publications

	Akron Baptist Temple Akron, Ohio	Highland Park Baptist Church Chattanooga, Tennessee	First Baptist Church Dallas, Texas	First Baptist Church Hammond, Indiana	Canton Baptist Temple Canton, Ohio
Total income per year — 1968	$1,061,236.04 We believe in tithing. No pledge.	$625,000 (church only)	$2,220,141	Over $500,000	$526,260.89
Gave to missions in 1968	$101,293.34 Every Sunday school dept. has a missionary $1,000.	50% to missions.	$815,919	$80,000	$101,612.94
Number of adult classes (age 18 and over)	3	21	153	10	2
Attendance of adults	College & Career 150 Young Adults 400 Dr. Billing- ton 2,200 — 2,750	2,050	2,699	Average 1,800	Young single adults — 250 Pastor's class — 1542. Total 1,79
Number of youth class age (12-17)	Age 12 - 20 classes 13 - 20 classes 14 - 20 classes Ages 15-17—1 class each. Total — 63	2 departments 30 classes	146	41	37 total classes. 35 Jr. Hi. classes 2 Sr. Hi. classes
Attendance at youth classes	1,018	356	1,024	500	507
Number of Children's classes (birth to 11).	177	10 departments 120 classes	122	21 departments 155 classes	119
Attendance of children's classes	1,952	1,210	1,266	1,700	1,201
Summer Camp Program	Ohio Baptist Acres. Belongs to church. 4th July Bible Conference. 9 weeks. 400 capacity.	Camp Joy owned by church. 2,181 campers attended last year. Many thru Union Gospel Mission (free).	Jr. Camp Intermediate Camp	Bill Rice Ranch	Cooperate with Baptist Bible Fel- lowship. Send to camps (1) age 6 (200). (2) age 9-13 (80). (3) Youth Camp (161). (4) colleg retreat (139).
Camp Attendance	2,115	2,181 campers 540 professions of faith.	975	200	580
VBS	None at present. Dropped for camp in 1967.	None	3,850 enrolled 10 days	Yes	6 day program with classes from nursery to Jr. Hi. A missionary offer ing of over $500 received.
VBS Literature	None	None	Southern Baptist Literature	Varied	Standard Publishers.
VBS Attendance	0	0	2,900	1,195	1,484
Club Activities (Pioneer girls, Christian Service Brigade, RA's, Boy Scouts, etc.	No club activities	None	Sunbeam's, G.A.'s, Y.W.A.'s, R.A.'s	Church has own girls organization, Lamplighters.	No club activities

Landmark Baptist Temple Cincinnati, Ohio	Temple Baptist Church Detroit, Mich.	First Baptist Church Van Nuys, Calif.	Thomas Road Baptist Church Lynchburg, Virginia	Calvary Temple Denver, Colorado
$597,000	$965,877.15	$1,046,606.78	$548,550.15 (including radio & TV income) $315,670.12 (church income only)	$869,475
Don't know	$236,561.68	$122,481.89	$74,550.00	$200,000
1 adult 1 college & career	9 adult 18 over 18 Y.P. Dept.	32	7	12
1,250	2,300	Attendance—920 Enrollment—1,257	1,300 (approx.)	1,173
7	12 — grade 6 12 — grade 7 12 — grade 8 12 — grade 9 18 — grades 10, 11 and 12.	51 Jr. Hi classes 27 Sr. Hi classes 78 — total	41	25
1,050		735	480 (approx.)	350
11 classes Don't divide	139	103	70	121
1,750 (approx.)	1,200	1,575	860 (approx.)	921
Ohio Baptist Fellowship. 3 camps — junior and senior hi.	Cooperate with Michigan Baptist Bible Fellowship camp in Ohio.	Recently purchased 26 acres for new camp development.	Owns and operates Treasure Island Youth Camp — 10 minutes from church.	Camp for each age — Primary, Junior, Jr. Hi, High school. Retreats for older groups.
1,000 plus	1,000	1,715	Expect 1500 - 2000 in 1969. 1,200 in 1968.	420
None	None — we are not a neighborhood church. People come great distance to church.	8 day program.	None	None
None	None	Scripture Press Southern Baptist	None	None
0	0	1,400	0	0
None	None	Heavy emphasis on clubs: Boy Scouts, Girl Scouts, Little League, Crafts, etc.	None	Pioneer Girls, Omega and Alpha Teens.

	Akron Baptist Temple Akron, Ohio	Highland Park Baptist Church Chattanooga, Tennessee	First Baptist Church Dallas, Texas	First Baptist Church Hammond, Indiana	Canton Baptis Temple Canton, Ohio
Organized recreation program	Church has it's own basketball league. Ten teams. Doesn't cooperate with other churches in sports.		Ministry to the whole man. Church has gyms large enough for two basketball games, a bowling alley, a skating rink, game room and exercise room.		Church has 3 b ketball leagues. 8 teams in each league. (1) age 12-14 (2) age 1 and up — single (3) Young married couples. 12 softball team
Attitude toward Baptism	Must be immersed as a believer to be member. Church has Baptism every 2 weeks.	A person is baptized immediately upon profession of faith.	A convert is immersed after he has a thorough understanding of Baptism.	Convert is baptized by immersion upon public proof of faith. Baptize every Sunday A.M. and P.M.	Must be baptize to be a member One of ministers makes a home c before person is baptized.
Number of Baptisms last year.	173	2,020	310	1,567	362
Attitude toward Evangelism	Preach for conversion every service.	Evangelism is the key to getting and holding the multitudes.	Christ is preached at main services. People are given an invitation to accept Christ. Evangelism is not finished till person is in life of church.	Preach for conversions every Sunday.	Gives an invitati each week. Weekly visitatior
Number of conversions last year	374	2,657	310 Baptisms	3,419	758 (conversior and membership
Promotion	Two contest days, Fall and Spring. No emphasis on special days one or two days per year. Homecoming is planned.	A layman is in charge of promotion each month. Special days are used to bring the lost to church. Contests are used. 5,000 contacts are made by church each week.	Morning worship is televised. Growth is centered around the individual Sunday school class. Church does not use Sunday school contest on a church wide basis, but will allow a contest within a department. Growth is built on education.	Heavy emphasis on promotion. Two Sunday school drives a year. A 12 week drive in the spring and another in the fall.	Only one contest last year for 3 weeks. Little em phasis on promotion or special days.
Next Goal in Attendance	6,500 for 1969 Trophy given to dept. with greatest growth.	To average 6,000 in Sunday school and double missionary giving.	Church believer enrollment is more important than attendance. If they are enlisted, they will attend.	1,800 in new building	
Next step in building plans	No building plans. Need to fill what we have.	Plan to build a sanctuary that will seat 5,500-6,000.			$350,000 building in 1969 to add 32,000 sq. ft.

Landmark Baptist Temple Cincinnati, Ohio	Temple Baptist Church Detroit, Mich.	First Baptist Church Van Nuys, Calif.	Thomas Road Baptist Church Lynchburg, Virginia	Calvary Temple Denver, Colorado
Inter-mural in Sunday school. Softball with YMCA church league, inter-city. 300 - 500 use park on Sunday afternoon.	Baseball league in summer.	Church has an organized basketball league.	Compete in city churches basketball league. We have gym at Treasure Island (our youth camp) located 10 miles from church. Gym being constructed at church presently.	Participate in city interchurch basketball and softball leagues.
Baptize immediately.	Scriptural Baptism is immersion of a believer in water.	Baptism by immersion for the believer.	Scriptural Baptism is immersion. Candidate for membership must first be scripturally baptized.	Baptism by immersion only. Not required for church membership. Emphasized for new converts.
860	Over 300	425	350	
Soul Winning.	The church places soul winning first on a list of priorities.	Preach and teach for conversion and dedication each service.	First in priorities. Invitation at every service.	Strong emphasis on evangelism within the sanctuary services balanced with personal evangelism on the part of the layman.
1,480	559 who came forward.	441	812 (in church services.)	Record is kept only of baptisms and membership.
Use promotional ideas. 3 large contests per year. Individual departments will have more. Ten special Sunday school drives — homecoming in Fall — 7,000 will attend. July 4th picnic. Sing Out — 6,000 will attend in August and Quartette (all night sing)	Very little emphasis on contest and promotion. Growth comes thru visitation and soul winning.	Visitation and activities. Radio broadcast of both services in morning. Strong music programming.	Two drives annually, Spring and Fall. Emphasis on soul winning, teaching and preaching.	Morning service televised live on nine channels — throughout Rocky Mt. Empire. Very little Sunday school promotion per se. Strong emphasis on necessity of Christian Education.
5,000 in Sunday school	Present educational space can handle 7,000.	3,333/week in Sunday school.	To average 3,000 plus in Sunday school during April-May-June, 1969.	Plan 14 buildings, one for each age group — and attendance to keep pace with building program.
Sanctuary 5,000	Just completed 4 million dollar building.	1.4 million educational and recreational complex in 1969.	Breaking ground now for new sanctuary seating 3,000 plus and 2 educational bldgs. with 44,000 sq. ft. of floor space.	Complete a Christian educational campus with a self-contained building for each Sunday school department.

	Akron Baptist Temple Akron, Ohio	Highland Park Baptist Church Chattanooga, Tennessee	First Baptist Church Dallas, Texas	First Baptist Church Hammond, Indiana	Canton Baptist Temple Canton, Ohio
Young People's Program	Saturday is youth program. Cooperate with other Fundamental Baptist churches. Films, speaker.	B.T.U. is held each Sunday evening.	Baptist Training Union on Sunday evenings.	Many youth activities every week.	Sunday evening musical program followed by Hi school students doing the speaking.
Literature	Y.F.C. within our Sunday afterglow	Provided by our staff.	Southern Baptist Publications	Church employs full-time director of literature to write lessons.	None
Attendance	0	3,000 in B.T.U.	2,000	200	90-100
Visitation Program	Four shifts of visitation. Not all come to organized program. 100 come to church. 400 go when time permits.	People go 2 by 2 to get people for Sunday school class. Visit absentees. Bus pastors visit.	Someone is responsible for each prospect.	Soul winning and absentee.	Tues. night, adult go calling. Sat. youth go calling. Heavy emphasis on absentee follow-up. Teachers do calling at their convenience
Number of lay people who visit each week	500	340	100 to 300	300	295
Number of calls made by layman each week	500 to 800	900	1200	1500	550
Average number of calls made by full time staff per week (does not include hospital and sick calls)	50	400	400	500	Home calls 100
Sunday School Buses	40 buses in past, but as people have cars — they are not needed. We built other churches that have made no need for buses.	Dr. Roberson meets with bus pastors every Saturday morning. Buses used for 3 main services.	Sunday school buses are used only with 6 missions. Ten years ago had much larger busing program than now in operation.	One-third of pupils are brought by bus. One of the major evangelistic outreaches. At present church has a growing bus ministry and plans to enlarge it.	Not a strong emphasis on Sunday school buses. Over half of those who ride buses adults.
Number of Sunday school buses	7	17	19 including VW's	62	5
Average weekly number reached by buses	220	620	220	1,500	205
Attitude toward cooperation with other churches	We are friendly. We speak to their Sunday school meeting. Will not cooperate with ministerial. Will cooperate with Evangelicals.	Does not cooperate with city ministerial, but fellowships with fundamental Baptist churches.	Cooperate with Southern Baptist churches. Dr. Criswell is president of SBC.	No cooperation with local ministerial. Cooperate with Bible believing only.	Will not cooperate with local ministerial or participate in cooperative evangelism.
Denomination	Baptist Bible Fellowship	Independent Baptist	SBC	Independent Baptist	Baptist Bible Fellowship

Landmark Baptist Temple Cincinnati, Ohio	Temple Baptist Church Detroit, Mich.	First Baptist Church Van Nuys, Calif.	Thomas Road Baptist Church Lynchburg, Virginia	Calvary Temple Denver, Colorado
Dept. meeting for Sunday school. *Graded.* Headed by Supt. Adult Scripture Training at 6:00 p.m. Bible memory. Choir rehearsal.	Jr. Hi, Sr. Hi and Y.P. meetings Sunday before church. Saturday night programs for Sr. Hi and young people.	Special program each Sunday for each age group.	We own and operate Treasure Island Youth Camp, located 10 min. from church. Take 3,000 plus young people each summer free. Also, T.V., etc.	Omega program Wednesday and Sunday evenings. Large house adjacent to the church is called Omega house. House is their own for week day activities.
None	None	Mixed	None	Success with Youth
0	0	Junior-College	1,500	BTU for up to 200
Thurs. A.M. and P.M. Go in teams. Team of 2 averages 4 calls. Call by S.S. dept. Not church wide visitation. Visit absentee and prospects and visitors.	Mon. night supper followed by visitation program on prospects, absentees, sick fellowship calls. Thurs. A.M. program for ladies and men who work the afternoon shift.	Five pastors responsible for visitation plus emphasis on Sunday school class visitation by members.	No organized night for visitation. Each S.S. worker must visit 2 hours weekly in homes. Each bus captain, 3 hrs. They usually do more. All are urged to participate.	Our staff divisional directors and pastors are responsible for all follow-up of prospects and absentees in their areas.
350	500	500	600	No total weekly record of lay visits is kept.
700	1,000	1,000	400	
100 (27 conversions by full time staff per wk.	50-60	100		200
Added 10 buses this year.	No great emphasis on bus ministry.	Our eight buses are used for recreation, day school, and social activities.	Just beginning bus ministry now. Running 15 buses now. Bring in about 500 per Sunday. Plan to enlarge to 30 buses this year with 1,000 weekly riders.	Buses are used primarily as shuttle buses connecting intercity routes for all services, church and Sunday school.
70	5	Buses not used for Sunday school.	15	3
1,680	200	None for Sunday school.	500	80
Not member of council of churches. Good fellowship with Evangelicals.	Cooperate only with fundamental Baptist churches.	Cooperation with most Evangelical groups.	No cooperation with local ministerial association.	We have a good working relationship with Council of churches and pastor serves on Board of Directors of the N.A.E., Denver Chapter.
Baptist Bible Fellowship	Baptist Bible Fellowship	Independent Baptist	Baptist Bible Fellowship	Interdenominational

	Akron Baptist Temple Akron, Ohio	Highland Park Baptist Church Chattanooga, Tennessee	First Baptist Church Dallas, Texas	First Baptist Church Hammond, Indiana	Canton Baptist Temple Canton, Ohio
Attitudes to separation from worldly influence	Complete separation required of Sunday school teachers. Preach against sinful practice.	Reflects a strict concept of separation from world.	Evident in individual lives.	Separated from worldly influence exhorted from pulpit, and demanded of Sunday school teachers.	Positive in preaching Christian living, but this includes separation from negative. Has a reputation for exhorting people to be separated from sinful amusements; dancing, social drinking, etc.
Second person most responsible for growth	Mr. Stanley Bond	Dr. J. R. Faulkner	12 age group directors.	None	Rev. Mel Sabaka

Landmark Baptist Temple Cincinnati, Ohio	Temple Baptist Church Detroit, Mich.	First Baptist Church Van Nuys, Calif.	Thomas Road Baptist Church Lynchburg, Virginia	Calvary Temple Denver, Colorado
Separation from worldly influences preached and expected of Sunday school teachers.	Preach separation from worldly influence.	Not a main emphasis. Separation is a positive attitude.	Separation from worldly influences preached. Demanded of all leaders, officers, teachers, etc.	Preaches Separation. Middle of the road approach.
Team Effort	Team Effort	Rev. Lowell Brown	Rev. James Soward, Jr.	None